✾ RUhAL ✾
RIDES

No 2: East Surrey

Country cycle rides
of adventure & discovery
for all the family

compiled & written
by
Ron Strutt

Credits: Text, photographs, and sketch maps are by Ron Strutt.

Vintage line drawings are by the late Duncan Moul from Picturesque Surrey, published in 1902 by F E Robinson & Co.

ISBN 1 85284 273 3

Published by Cicerone Press, 2 Police Square, Milnthorpe, Cumbria LA7 7PY

Ron Strutt

Welcome!

to the second volume in the *Rural Rides* series of cycle rides. Once again, we have put together a collection of rides through some of the most beautiful and varied scenery that Surrey has to offer. There are rides here to suit every level of cycling experience, and all of them will take you to fascinating places you probably never knew existed, many of them inaccessible by car.

The spectacular heights of the Surrey Hills, the rolling downland of the north of the county, and the lonely, low-lying fields of the Weald – where else could you find such a rich variety of landscape within a few miles. A host of delightful small towns and quiet villages mean there's plenty to explore, and you're sure to be tempted by some of the welcoming country pubs along the way.

We can certainly promise that you'll see more of nature than most other people will see in half a lifetime: deer, foxes, squirrels, countless rabbits, and many other creatures – not in an artificial setting, not at a distance, but close to, in their natural habitat.

We are so lucky to be surrounded by such wonderful countryside, and with this guide and a bike you can really make the most of it.

About the original Rural Rides...

Rural Rides was the name given by William Cobbett to an account of his series of journeys on horseback across much of southern England in the years between 1821 and 1830. Cobbett was a countryman – he was born at Farnham, in Surrey – as well as a leading radical politician. He was deeply distrustful of the findings of a government commission on agriculture, and decided to find out for himself the state of things in the countryside. His *Rural Rides* were the result, initially as a series of reports in Cobbett's own periodical *The Weekly Political Register* and later as a book.

Cobbett particularly chose to go on horseback and to keep away from the main roads:

> *"...my object was, not to see inns and turnpike-roads, but to see the country: to see the farmers at home, and to see the labourers in the fields; and to do this you must go either on foot or on horse-back. With a gig you cannot get about amongst bye-lanes and across fields, through bridleways and hunting-gates; and to tramp it is too slow, leaving the labour out of the question, and that is not a trifle."*

> written at Chilworth, near Guildford, Surrey Wednesday, 25th September, 1822

If Cobbett were alive today and repeating his travels, we think he would have chosen to use a bike, for that would be the ideal way for him to see today's countryside. And although motorways and trunk roads with their service areas and Happy Eaters may have taken over from the turnpike-roads and their coaching inns, Cobbett would still recognise the quiet country lanes, the byways, and bridleways which he travelled then and which you will follow on the rides in this guide.

Acknowledgements

Once again, I could not have completed this book without the encouragement and help of so many people.

Martin Smethurst has done another splendid job of editing the text for me, for which I am immensely grateful. When writer's block strikes or strange errors creep in, it is a great comfort to know there is someone who will make sense of your words.

Keith Dean has continued to drive me on to finish these books, and has run a one-man publicity campaign on my behalf. I sometimes wonder if, had it not been for him, I might have given up when the task seemed endless.

Once again, I owe so much to my wife Liz. She had a major operation while I was working on this book, so she could not join me on many of the rides. Instead, she waited patiently in the car, often for hours on end, while I roamed the Surrey countryside.

Throughout the time I have worked on these books she has done everything I could have wished to help and support me. No-one could ask for a better partner.

Contents

The Rides

Key to Rides

*Some (optional) parts of these rides are strenuous

Abbreviations used

FL	Fork left	BW	Bridleway
FR	Fork right	BY	Byway
L	Left	CP	Car park
R	Right	FP	Footpath
SO	Straight on	SP	Signpost(ed)
THL	Turn hard left	TJ	T-Junction
THR	Turn hard right	XR	Cross roads
TL	Turn left	XT	Cross tracks
TR	Turn right	XW	Cross ways

About the Rides

The Rural Rides series of cycling guides are for people who want to go cycling for leisure and enjoyment. Our aim in writing them has been to introduce greater numbers of ordinary people, including families with children, to the joys of exploring the countryside on a bike.

These rides are not intended to be races or endurance tests – there are no prizes for completing them in the least possible time. We want you to get out into the countryside, to explore it, and to enjoy all it has to offer. There is absolutely nothing to be gained (but much to be missed) by rushing along, so don't worry if you find that your speed is averaging only a few miles an hour. That's about right on these rides!

For newcomers

If you are taking up cycling for the first time, or coming back to it after a long absence, start with a few rides of four or five miles near to home and then begin with some of the shorter rides in this guide. Don't put yourself off by trying to do too much at first. Give yourself time and, with a little practice, you'll soon be ready and eager to tackle longer routes.

Some of the rides involve hill climbing, but don't let that deter you. Surrey has magnificent scenery to offer, especially in the south of the county, but the best views are to be had from the tops of hills! You have to put a bit of effort into getting up there, but it's worth it. Don't worry about hills – if you want to get off and walk up, then do so. Relax and enjoy it. Take time to appreciate the scenery unfolding around you and to anticipate the exhilarating downhill ride to come. It's no admission of defeat to walk up a hill; there are few cyclists who haven't had to do it at one time or another, and besides, walking with your bike as well as riding it is good exercise.

Getting to the Rides

By car

Cycle carriers designed to fit onto the backs or roofs of cars mean you are no longer restricted to rides which start in your immediate locality. If you don't have one of your own, some cycle shops now hire them. You can also buy cycle carriers which fit onto roof bars; look for a set designed for your make of car.

All of our rides begin at places where you can park your car while you go cycling. However, since the rides are circular, you can start from almost any point on the route. But if you do, please don't leave your car where it might cause inconvenience; remember that you could be away for some time. In particular, don't park in front of gates leading into farm fields or woodlands, even if they look as if they're rarely used. If you want to park in a pub car park, or on any other private land, ask the owner for permission first.

By train

Once upon a time the favourite way of cycling in distant parts was to travel there by train with your bike in the guard's van, and this is still the most environmentally-friendly way of doing it. Our directions and maps show the location of stations which are on or close to the rides. However, it is a sad fact that some of the latest designs of trains have either limited or non-existent facilities for bikes. For example, the trains operated by South West Trains on the Waterloo–Salisbury–Exeter line, most InterCity and some Regional Railways trains will take only two bikes at a time, and you must make reservations in advance at a cost of £3 each per single journey. This is hardly ideal for families or groups, or for a spur-of-the-moment outing!

Furthermore, the railways are in a state of major change at present, and we advise prospective rail-users to check the up-to-date situation in advance. In addition, if you are travelling at the weekend, check to see if trains are diverted because of work on the lines – bikes are not carried on replacement buses. For peak-hour journeys within the commuter area (roughly 30 miles from London) bikes are not allowed on London-bound trains in the morning and back in the evening.

On the plus side, where there are no restrictions, bikes normally travel free (at the time of writing). Just label them with your name and destination. For all rail enquiries telephone 0345 48 49 50.

Cycling on and off the road

The rides in this book make use of both surfaced roads and unmade tracks. Properly surfaced roads obviously make for easier and faster cycling, but most people find little fun in riding in the midst of traffic. On the other hand, cycling through deep mud isn't everyone's idea of the perfect day out, so we have tried to reach a reasonable compromise.

Our rides use country roads and lanes wherever possible, but we have tried to avoid those which are too busy or where the traffic tends to be very fast-moving. In the main, we have followed the cyclist's old maxim "Stick to the yellow", referring to the minor roads coloured yellow on Ordnance Survey maps. These roads are normally fairly quiet, but you must still take care because they can get busy at certain times.

We have used paths and tracks to bypass busy stretches of road or to take you into scenic or peaceful areas of countryside which are inaccessible by car. In Surrey, which has one of the highest rates of car ownership in the UK, few roads are ever completely peaceful in the way that byways and bridleways can be.

However, off-road tracks can sometimes be in poor condition. Some people will not mind this but others will – one person's nightmare of mud and filth is another's excitement and challenge!

The route details tell you where problems are most likely to arise and, where possible, we suggest diversions along surfaced roads so that you have a choice.

Off-road cycling

Most off-road tracks are unsurfaced and their condition can vary enormously. Some can be muddy after wet weather, but in summer they should give few problems. Conversely, there are parts of Surrey where the ground is very sandy, and the going can be hard when it is dry. In both cases, tracks which are regularly used by horses can be challenging.

If a particular path is very bad, it may be worth contacting the County Council to see if they can make repairs. Budgets for this kind of work are limited, but something may be done if enough people complain. (Better still, volunteer to spend the odd weekend helping to look after Surrey's rights of way; contact the Environment Unit, Planning Dept, County Hall, Kingston-upon-Thames, KT1 2DT).

We have checked the rides in this guide in a variety of conditions, and most of the off-road tracks should not give you any problems in reasonable weather. There are a few places where you may have to walk your bike, but there is always a good reason for the ride being routed that way.

The majority of bikes sold today are all-terrain or 'mountain' bikes and can cope with some fairly difficult off-road conditions. On the other hand, there is no reason why you shouldn't use a road bike providing you're sensible. You may have to get off and push more often, and you must be careful not to damage your bike. If your own bike is not suitable for these rides you can hire one designed for off-road use. You must decide whether conditions are too difficult for the bike you are using. We cannot accept any responsibility for damage done to a bike as a result of using it on one of the rides in this guide.

Riding on off-road tracks means keeping in a low gear so you can cope with sudden problems or changes in conditions. Keep both hands on the handlebars at all times, make sure you are totally in control of your bike, and keep your speed down. Be especially careful of dry sand or gravel surfaces which can cause you to skid or lose your balance; mud and wet chalk can also be treacherously slippery. If mud builds up under your mudguards (if you have them) it can jam your wheels solid, so make sure you clear it out before that happens.

The simple answer is that if conditions become too difficult, get off and walk. Just as with climbing hills, there is nothing to say that you have to stay in the saddle all the time. Walking with your bike will allow you to enjoy the countryside all the more, and you will certainly see more wildlife. In any case, we happen to think

Studying the route

that walking with a bike can be as much fun as riding it (and good exercise), so be prepared for a little footwork on our rides!

The other point to remember about off-road tracks is that in summer they're often lined with nettles, brambles, and other unsociable vegetation. It's a good idea to cover bare skin with sleeves, long trousers and socks; you may not want to wear them all the time, but having them with you in case you need them may save a lot of discomfort. It also makes sense to carry ointment to treat stings.

Following the routes

For each ride there is a 'Route in Brief' opposite the map, followed by a more complete and readable description of the ride and the places of interest along the way. You can choose which you prefer to use as your guide.

The distances in the text give you a rough idea of how far you've cycled. They are approximate and are for interest, not precise navigation. In a few places where we think you might have problems with the route, we have put up small 'Rural Rides' waymark signs.

We have taken a great deal of care to ensure that our information is as accurate as possible but changes do happen with great regularity and surprising speed. If you discover any that have taken place since this guide went to press we would be delighted to hear from you.

The Maps

The sketch maps in this guide are intended to give basic information about the routes and the places along the way. To get the most out of your ride we recommend that cyclists and walkers should use the Ordnance Survey maps.

These come in two types: the Landranger series in illustrated red card covers at a scale of 1:50000 (roughly 1¼ inches to the mile) and the green-coloured Pathfinder series at a scale of 1:25000 (or 2½ inches to the mile). The Landranger maps cover a wider area on each sheet, which can be useful on long trips, but the Pathfinder maps give you much more detailed information.

(The new Explorer series of maps, in orange covers, is gradually replacing the Pathfinders. They use the same 1:25000 scale but cover a much greater area.)

Facilities

Pubs, shops, refreshment facilities, toilets, and public telephones are shown on the maps in those areas where they are not very plentiful. In most towns and larger villages, readers should be able to find them without difficulty.

Pubs, Inns and Hotels

There are some absolutely delightful pubs and inns along the routes of these rides, and it can often be very difficult deciding which one (or ones) to call into.

The recent liberalisation of the licensing laws should increasingly prove a boon to the cyclist. Quite a few of the pubs referred to in these rides are now opening their doors from 11am through to 11pm (10.30pm on Sundays), so you don't have to ride with one eye on your watch if you're looking forward to that refreshing pint halfway round.

Although many pubs are sticking to the 'standard' opening times for the time being, a good number are experimenting with longer hours, and a steady trade from the cycling fraternity at a nice rural pub may well help to influence the situation in the long term. In the meantime, we have given times of opening and food service in the pub entries only if they differ substantially from the 'standard' hours of 11am to either 2.30 or 3pm, 6pm to 11pm (noon to 3pm, 7pm to 10.30pm on Sundays).

Many rural pubs pride themselves on a variety of real ales and a high standard of homemade food, several serving excellent Sunday lunches, though if you want to be certain a pub is open or that food is available we advise you to telephone in advance. And do remember, the cyclist is subject to the same laws on alcohol consumption as any other road-user.

The codes relating to pub facilities are as follows:

C: has a Children's Certificate or a room where children under 14 are allowed
G: has a garden
Food: serves bar meals or snacks – can be anything from sandwiches to full meals

Rest: has a restaurant with waiter/ waitress service
Acc: provides accommodation

Shops

In rural areas, general shops and off-licences, where you can at least buy a can of drink or snacks, are shown on the maps or listed in the text. However, most rural shops have closed in recent years and there is no guarantee that those shown on the maps will still be there (although your custom will help those which remain). Bear in mind that many rural shops close at 5.30pm, have half-day closing, and don't open on Sundays.

Most petrol stations now include a small shop. They are usually open until late and on Sundays, and often provide toilet facilities as well. Where they provide the only such facilities in an area we have marked them on the maps.

Enjoying the countryside

Useful information

When to go cycling

Cycling isn't just a summer activity – the rest of the year has much to offer. Indeed, the cooler weather of spring and autumn can be more comfortable for cycling than the heat of summer, and even winter cycling can be great fun providing you dress appropriately and the roads are free from ice.

The countryside is beautiful whatever the time of year, so why not get out and enjoy it. In winter when the trees and hedges are bare of leaves you can see much more of the view. In spring the clear air is perfect for distant vistas, and the ground becomes a carpet of fresh green growth and flowers. In autumn the colours of the leaves can add a spectacular new dimension to many familiar scenes.

What to wear

There are two key rules as to what to wear on a bike. The first is to wear layers of clothes so that you can easily add or take off just the right amount for comfort; the choice between a thin cotton shirt and a thick woollen sweater is really no choice at all.

If you set out on a warm summer's day in just a T-shirt, always have a couple of extra layers with you. A hot day can turn very cool if it clouds over, and even in Surrey there are places where it can become quite inhospitable in bad weather.

The second rule is to ensure that what you wear below the waist is not going to chafe the more delicate parts of your anatomy. If you cycle only occasionally, the cost of lycra cycling shorts may seem excessive, but they really do have benefits. They have no rough seams, they move with the body rather than rub against it, and they dry quickly if they get wet. Worn without underwear, they are lined with chamois (the best) or a synthetic material (cheaper) which absorbs perspiration, prevents chafing, and provides extra padding between you and the saddle. They are definitely recommended. Their only drawback is that they don't protect your legs against nettles and the like. You can get long 'tights', but wearing light cotton trousers over lycra shorts, while not ideal, is better than getting your legs stung.

In winter your legs can get very cold. One solution is to wear thermal long johns under trousers, but we have found that a pair of light cotton pyjama trousers worn as under-trousers provides an excellent added layer of insulation which can cope with quite cold temperatures. Jeans are totally unsuitable for cycling. They are stiff and unyielding, with prominent seams in all the wrong places, and if they get wet they can be extremely heavy and uncomfortable.

You will need gloves more often than you may think. Hands can get cold and numb very quickly on a bike, even if the rest of you is warm. Special cycling gloves with shock-absorbing pads are available, but ordinary thermal gloves offer good protection in all but the coldest weather and are thin enough not to be cumbersome.

There has been much debate about the value and desirability of wearing cycle helmets. There is evidence to suggest they may give a feeling of security to wearers which encourages them to take more risks. Many wearers also seem to think that helmets give them more protection than they actually do. If you ride in heavy traffic, where the risk to you from other people's mistakes is much greater, you should probably wear a helmet. Children and novices, who have not yet developed their cycling skills and their ability to handle potentially dangerous situations, should always wear helmets. However, they must still learn to ride sensibly and not to take risks.

If you don't wear a helmet, you'll need a hat most of the time. On hot days you'll want one to prevent your head burning, but it mustn't make your head too warm. In cool weather you want a hat which will not only keep your head warm but your ears too. Whatever type of headgear you wear, make sure it will stay securely on your head. You won't be able to control your bike properly if you're trying to hang on to a hat.

Eye protection is vital, not just for bright sun but also to keep insects out of your eyes. Fashionable, if expensive, reflective visors can be bought from any cycle shop, but a good pair of sunglasses will do as well, provided their frames do not block your peripheral vision. You may want to wear them even in low light (there are a lot of insects at dusk on summer evenings), so consider glasses which adjust to match the light.

Rain need not be a problem on one-day rides like those in this guide. If heavy or continuous rain seems likely, we suggest you postpone your ride, but light showers need not bother you if there is some form of shelter nearby, and it can even be refreshingly pleasant to ride through light rain on a hot day. The problem comes if you want (or have) to push on through heavier showers.

Ordinary rainwear is excellent at keeping moisture out, but it is also very good at keeping it in. If you are prepared to stop for the duration of the rain (even if there is little shelter), ordinary cheap rainwear such as a light nylon jacket will suffice. Otherwise, you will need a waterproof of a type which allows sweat to escape (they can be quite expensive) or a traditional cycling cape.

Capes cost less, are naturally ventilated, and roll up into a fairly small space for carrying. Their main drawback is that wind or the draught of passing traffic can make the bike hard to control.

Never wear a rain garment with a hood while cycling. They dangerously restrict your ability to see to the side and rear and can muffle the sound of approaching vehicles.

Weather protection

In summer, and sometimes even in spring and autumn, you'll need to make sure your bare arms, legs and face are well-coated with suntan lotion. It is sometimes easy to forget that you can be out in the open sun for a long time on a bike ride, and the cooling breeze can be deceptive. Exposed skin can get burned before you realise it. Take the suntan lotion with you to top up your protection during the day.

What to take

If you are going out on any length of ride, you will want some means of carrying spare clothing, waterproofs, and other essential items. Small rucksacks or backpacks can be bought quite cheaply, but they are not ideal. Apart from the fact that the weight of the contents can soon mount up, your back will get unpleasantly hot under a pack. The answer is a set of front or back panniers, or a saddlebag. You don't want to look as if you're setting off on an expedition to the upper reaches of the Amazon, but there are a few things it is sensible to take with you in addition to spare clothing:

- a small first aid kit with a couple of plasters and some antiseptic cream to treat minor cuts and grazes
- a basic repair kit, including a puncture repair outfit, a set of tyre levers, an adjustable spanner, small screwdrivers and a cycle pump with connectors to fit the valves on all the group's bikes. Many people take a spare inner tube to save fixing a puncture out on the road
- food and drink: you always feel hungry and thirsty when you're miles from the nearest source of supplies; on a hot day you will be surprised how much liquid you need, and if it's cold you will need to eat more to keep warm
- a wet cloth in a plastic bag, a dry rag, and a few tissues
- a roll of insulating tape – it seems the kind of thing which is sure to come in handy one day
- a notebook and pen

A group of cyclists can, of course, divide some of these things between them.

Rights of Way

Cyclists have a legal right to ride on all public roads (except motorways and places where traffic signs indicate otherwise) and on those rights of way (but only those) which are classified as:

- bridleways (but not Permissive Horse Rides)
- byways open to all traffic (BOATs)
- roads used as public paths (RUPPs)
- the delightfully-named 'Carriage Roads used mainly as Bridleways' (CRBs)
- designated cycle tracks
- cross-country footpaths or tracks in Scotland

Rights of way are sometimes indicated by coloured arrows or waymarks to indicate their status; blue for bridleways and red for byways or RUPPs. (Yellow arrows indicate footpaths.) Even when you have a right of way as a cyclist, you must always give way to walkers and horses, for your safety as much as theirs.

Cycling is allowed on most canal and river towpaths – check the bylaws of the relevant navigation authority. On British Waterways' canals you need a BW Cycling Permit.

Except in Scotland, cyclists and horse riders have no right to use public footpaths. *Nor* do they have the right to ride across areas such as heaths, commons and woods, even on the tracks which cross them, unless those tracks are bridleways or byways, or when permission has been specifically given. The fact that the public has access to an area makes no difference to this; access is for walking only. Cycling on footpaths and open areas constitutes trespass, and the landowner could sue you. This might sound far-fetched, but it could be a serious possibility if you cause damage.

Beyond that, a local council can ban cyclists from particular footpaths, or even bridleways, if it feels that they are causing a nuisance, and it is then an offence to ignore the ban. In the past, few people were ever prosecuted for this offence but, with the introduction of fixed penalty 'on-the-spot' fines, the police in many areas are beginning to crack down. It is also usually an offence under local bylaws to cycle on public open areas such as commons or the tracks that cross them (if they are not rights of way).

Bikes can do tremendous damage to the countryside, so please, never ride on unauthorised paths or open areas, and even if you are on a bridleway, if you think you might be damaging the path or its surroundings, dismount and walk.

This may sound like an awful lot of legal dos and don'ts aimed at restricting your enjoyment of the countryside, but there is a serious point to it. Cyclists won the right to use bridleways only through the 1968 Countryside Act. Many ramblers, horse riders, and country residents would like to see that right taken away, with cyclists being limited to the roads once more, and the pressure groups which represent these people have a lot of influence.

The actions of a small number of stupid or inconsiderate cyclists who refuse to stick to reasonable rules could result in off-road cycling being banned for everyone.

In one or two instances, our routes do follow footpaths, but only where they offer the only realistic alternative to riding on busy roads. Where this happens you must dismount and walk; in most cases only short distances are involved.

Rights of way matters are generally the responsibility of county councils (or, where they exist, unitary councils), although in some cases they may be handled by borough, district, or even parish councils. If you find a right of way in Surrey that is blocked, is in poor condition, which is not signposted where it meets a public road, or which needs waymarking along its route, contact Surrey County Council Rights of Way Section on 0181-541 9331 or 01483 519331 in the first instance.

Rights of way are shown on most Ordnance Survey maps, but there may occasionally have been changes since the map was printed.

The Law for Cyclists

Traffic restrictions such as one-way systems, prohibited turns, and many other requirements of the law and the Highway Code apply as much to cyclists as to drivers of motor vehicles. Strictly speaking, the restrictions apply even if you are wheeling your bike, but a dismounted cyclist acting in a sensible manner is unlikely to get into trouble.

The situation is less clear if you're riding your bike though. In some places cyclists are expected (even by the police) to ignore restrictions clearly not aimed at them. In other places the law is rigidly enforced. The main problem, though, is one of safety. Other road-users may not expect you to make a banned movement – such as riding the wrong way in a one-way street – and an accident could result.

It is an offence under the 1972 Road Traffic Act to ride recklessly, carelessly, or under the influence of drink or drugs. This applies to cyclists on bridleways and cycle paths as well as public roads.

Insurance

There is no legal requirement for cyclists in the UK to have insurance, but it is a good idea to make sure you are covered, not just against the possible theft of your bike, but also for injury and damage which may result from an accident in which you are involved. If you swerve to avoid a hazard and cause a car which is passing to collide with someone else, or if you hit a pedestrian, you could be sued and be bankrupted if you don't have insurance cover.

Some household contents insurance policies cover such matters as cycle theft and personal liability to third parties, but there may be restrictions as to which members of the family are covered and in what circumstances, so check the fine print. There are also specialist insurance policies for cyclists – see an insurance broker for information.

Safety

Many people are put off cycling because they think it is dangerous in today's traffic conditions. In fact, the chances of having an accident and being injured are really very small. You can reduce the risks still further (and increase your enjoyment of cycling at the same time) by improving your skills in cyclecraft. Books such as *Cyclecraft* by John Franklin (published by Unwin Paperbacks, 1988) contain a great deal of valuable guidance, or you can enrol on a cycle safety course (ask your council or police road safety officer for details). The notes given here are no substitute for either.

The routes in this guide avoid main roads as far as possible, but it is important to remember that few roads in Surrey are completely quiet. Even on country lanes you will come across motorists who do not expect you to be there. Keep to the proper side of the road, and make sure you are fully in control of your bike at all times. Always wear clothing that makes you easily and quickly visible to the motorist. The driver of an approaching car may have only seconds to realise you are there, and bright colours draw attention to your presence. High-visibility jackets also seem to encourage drivers to give you more room when overtaking.

It may seem strange advice, but it is not a good idea to ride too close to the side of the road. It can be more difficult for motorists to see you there, you are more likely to encounter obstacles, and you have no room to manoeuvre in case of emergency. You will also find that motorists will be more inclined to squeeze past you in dangerous circumstances. Some less experienced cyclists ride close to the edge of the road because they feel guilty about getting in the way of the traffic and, sadly, that seems only to reinforce the prejudices of some drivers. The law is quite clear. A cyclist has as much right to be on the road as any other road-user, and if you are in front you have the right of precedence. The fact that you are slower than the rest of the traffic has no bearing on the matter – when did you ever see a tractor driver who worried about going slowly?

Obviously, you must not obstruct the free flow of traffic by negligence or mis-behaviour (as the law puts it), but that doesn't mean you have to keep out of the way of, or constantly give way to, other vehicles. You should allow them to overtake, but only where it is safe and reasonable. However, having said that, you must judge each situation sensibly.

Most drivers are considerate to cyclists and will overtake only when it is safe, but a few can make life unpleasant. It is tempting to insist on your rights, but it isn't worth it. You will only antagonise them – and you're the vulnerable one. Give in with grace. In general, if the traffic is building up behind you, it is often better to stop and let it pass, if only because it's not much fun riding along with a queue of impatient cars on your back wheel.

In a few places our rides have to venture onto busy roads. Don't be put off by this; even on the busiest of roads you will come to no harm if you ride sensibly and take care. In fact busier roads tend to be wider, giving you more room to keep clear of the traffic.

Whatever you read elsewhere (even in the Highway Code), it is not a good idea to ride two abreast, especially on narrow roads. You will constantly have to drop back into single file to let other vehicles pass, and, while riding abreast is very sociable, your attention may be distracted from a possible hazard. If you are riding with children, there must always be an adult behind them and, ideally, one in front as well.

Always carry lights on your bike and use them whenever the light is poor. It's better to waste a set of batteries than risk an accident through not being seen. Don't leave your lights at home because you expect to be back before dusk – you may be delayed.

The Country Code

In the country, whether you're a cyclist, walker or motorist, always abide by the Country Code:

- Guard against fire risks
- Fasten all gates
- Keep dogs under proper control
- Keep to paths across farmland
- Avoid damaging fences, hedges and walls
- Leave no litter
- Safeguard water supplies
- Protect wildlife, wild plants and trees

- Go carefully on country roads
- Respect the life of the countryside

Cycling and Animals

Cycling in the country means you're bound to meet animals of various types. Most of them will be in fields, or otherwise out of harm's way, but some of them will be in your path, occasionally with disconcerting results.

Many horses get worried about bikes. We don't recommend trying to overtake a horse on a track, but if you are keeping your speed down the situation will rarely arise. If you have to overtake a horse on the road, make sure the rider knows you are there and is fully in control. Then pass at a reasonable speed, giving the horse plenty of room. If a horse is coming towards you on a narrow road or track, stop and let it pass. If the horse seems

The delights of cycling – leafy lanes winding through the countryside.

particularly agitated it may help if you dismount.

If a herd of cows is heading along the road in the same direction as you, don't try to overtake or push through. Wait for them to turn off. If you meet a herd coming towards you, back off. Whatever you do, never try to push past or let them push past you.

Dogs love cyclists and will often charge at you (usually in fun) the moment they see you. The best advice is usually to stop, especially if the owner is present to bring it under control. The problem is that a dog leaping around can make you swerve or even send you crashing to the ground. Fortunately they seem to lose interest as soon as you stop.

Most other animals, especially wild ones, will scatter as soon as they see or hear you but they may dart across your path, so slow down and be prepared to stop.

Wildfowl will sometimes react in this way, but often they will continue on their way regardless of your presence. Stop and let them get out of the way before you proceed. From time to time, especially on canal or river towpaths you will come across larger birds such as swans who simply refuse to move. They need to be treated with respect, especially if they have young. Dismount and edge round them, keeping the bike between you and the bird.

Geese can be very aggressive and may chase you if they don't like the look of you. This can be quite an unnerving experience, and a hasty withdrawal to a discreet distance seems the best advice!

Find out more about Surrey

If you enjoy these rides you may want to discover more about the many different aspects of the county. There are hundreds of books about Surrey, its towns and villages, but we have listed some of the best to look out for. Most are available from libraries throughout the county and many good booksellers have a local interest section.

Highways & Byways in Surrey by Eric Parker (Macmillan, 2nd edition 1935): this wonderful book is long out of print but it can be borrowed from libraries – well worth reading.

Surrey: a County History by John Janaway (Countryside Books, 1995): an extremely readable account of the story of Surrey from ancient to modern times.

Hidden Surrey by Chris Howkins (Countryside Books, 1987): begins where most guide books leave off. (There is a companion volume *Hidden Surrey – Town & Country* for the towns and larger villages.)

Portrait of Surrey by Basil E Cracknell (Robert Hale, 2nd edition 1974): a picture of the county in words as its title suggests.

All Surrey towns and most of the villages have at least one history or guide book. The Local Studies section in Guildford Library has an impressive collection of them, many of which are available on loan to members of any branch of the Surrey County Libraries.

THE RIDES

Here are hill and dell in endless variety. Here are the chalk and the
sand, vieing with each other in making beautiful scenes. Here is a
navigable river and fine meadows. Here are woods and downs. Here is
something of everything but fat marshes and their skeleton-making
agues.

Those that travel on turnpike roads know nothing of England.
Against a great road things are made for show. Here we see the people
without any disguise or affectation. And here we gain real knowledge
as to their situation.

William Cobbett

Key to Maps

▶ Direction of main route   ▷ Alternative route (see text)

③ etc Stage of route (see text)

Road   Dual Carriageway or Motorway

Bridleway or Track   Footpath

River or Canal   Stream

Railway Line
with Station

Public House

Shop (for general provisions)

Petrol station with shop

Light refreshments

Car park (charge may be payable)

Toilets (charge may be payable)

Place of Interest

Notable Building

School

Viewpoint

Golf course

Church

Public telephone

Radio or TV mast

Castle

Army camp, training area or range

Level crossing

Bridge

Traffic lights

Ride A:
Wealden Woodlands

Forest Green • Ewhurst • Ellens Green • Oakwood Hill • Paynes Green • Vann
Lake • Ockley • Wallis Wood • Lyefield • Forest Green

Distance:	21½ miles
Landranger Maps:	187
Pathfinder Maps:	1226 and 1246

Nearly 200 years ago William Cobbett said that only three things grew well on
the Weald clay – grass, wheat and oak trees. It remains just as true today. At
one time much of the Weald was deep forest and many of the local villages
and farmsteads – Forest Green, Ewhurst, Oakwood, Wallis Wood, Gosterwood
and countless others – can relate their names directly to their woodland
origins.

The scenery is splendid, with idyllic cottages and farmhouses dotted about the
fields and woods, and there are plenty of pubs along the wayside to welcome
the thirsty or weary rider. Most of the roads and paths are lined by trees and
hedges, giving protection from the blazing sun and wind alike, but still allowing
views over open fields beyond. This must be one of the most delightful cycle
rides in all Surrey!

Bridleways in the Weald can be hard work for cyclists, but fortunately this part
of Surrey has plenty of narrow country lanes which are all but traffic-free, so
we have made only limited use of off-road tracks on this ride. Equally fortunately,
there are no real hills to speak of, so climbs tend to be either long and gradual
or steep but short, making the ride ideal for almost any cyclist. The full ride is
21 miles long but, taken at an easy pace, it doesn't seem a long way, and with
such peaceful countryside to enjoy, few should have any difficulty in completing
the route. However, because it loops around a fairly compact area, you can
always take a short-cut to reduce the length of the journey if you wish.

Starting Points

As in some other parts of the Surrey
Weald, parking facilities are limited for
this ride.

The most obvious place is at Forest Green
(grid reference TQ 120412), where an
area outside the church may be
convenient except, of course, during
Sunday services. Some of the pubs on the
ride may allow customers to leave their
cars, but ask first. Other than that, some
of the local roads have broad verges.
However, parking is forbidden on the
green at Ockley.

If you don't mind an extra 4 miles cycling,
including a steep climb at the end of the
ride, there are car parks on the slopes of
Leith Hill. To reach them from Forest
Green, follow the B2126 Holmbury road

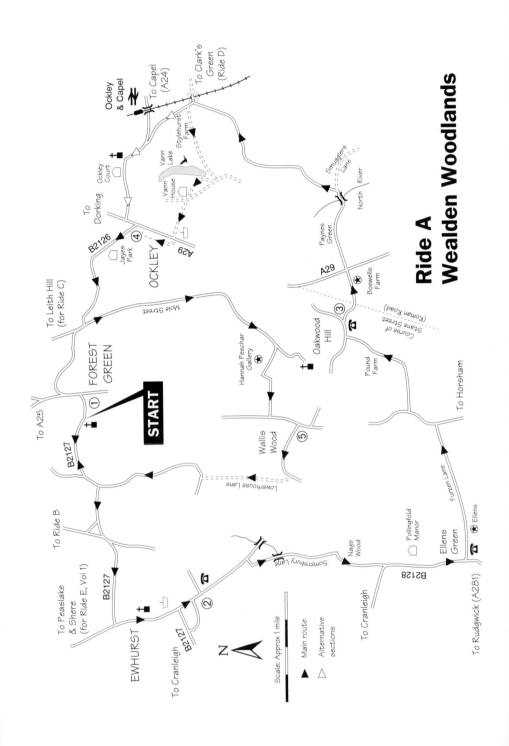

Ride A
Wealden Woodlands

Scale: Approx 1 mile

N

▲ Main route
△ Alternative sections

Ockley & Capel — To Capel (A24), To Clark's Green (Ride D), Stylehurst Farm, Vann Lake, Vann House, Ockley Court, To Dorking, Smugglers Lane, North River, Paynes Green, Boswells Farm, A29, A29, B2126, ④, Jayes Park, OCKLEY, Mole Street, To Leith Hill (for Ride C), Hannah Peschar Gallery, Oakwood Hill, ③, Course of Stane Street (Roman Road), Pound Farm, To Horsham, FOREST GREEN, ①, To A25, START, B2127, Wallis Wood, ⑤, Lowerhouse Lane, To Ride B, B2127, Nags Wood, Pollingfold Manor, Ellens Green, B2128, ⊕ Ellens, To Cranleigh, Furzen Lane, To Rudgwick (A281), To Peaslake & Shere (for Ride E, Vol 1), B2127, EWHURST, ②, To Cranleigh, Somersbury Lane, To Cranleigh and take the first turning on the right – Tanhurst Lane. At the top is a National Trust car park (non-members pay a small fee), and a free one a short distance further on.

Alternatively, you can park in Cranleigh. From there it's only a couple of miles along the B2127 to Ewhurst.

⇌ The nearest station is at Ockley (Connex South Central). Turn right out of the station approach onto the B2126 and go under the bridge; Ockley village is about a mile away. Services have varied on this line in recent years, so be sure to check in advance. At the time of writing there are hourly trains off-peak on weekdays and Saturdays, but none on Sundays. The last trains are soon after 7pm (6pm on Saturdays).

The Route in Brief

① From Forest Green take the B2127 to Ewhurst, then TL at TJ by Bulls Head Inn. At far end of village continue SO into Horsham Lane (SP Ellens Green & Horsham) when Cranleigh road bends R.

② About 450 yds after cricket ground TR into Somersbury Lane, SP Ellens Green & Rudgwick. At TJ with B2128 TL. At Ellens Green, 400 yds after Wheatsheaf pub, TL into Furzen Lane. At far end of lane TL, SP Ewhurst & Oakwood Hill, then keep SO to Oakwood Hill. TR at TJ opposite Okewood Manor.

③ TR soon after Punchbowl pub into unsigned lane (Ruckmans Lane) then SO over A29 into Paynes Green Road. Continue SO for over 2 miles until L bend by Sherwood Cottage. Immediately after bend TL into Vann Lake Road (BW) at Stylehurst Farm. When lane divides take L branch (SO). Keep SO when tarred drive ends and becomes track then narrow

path. At TJ with another BW TR down slope and cross bridge. At top of short climb TR between cast-iron gateposts. At end of path take driveway opposite gates of Vann House and continue SO into Friday Street.

At A29 go SO onto gravelled track past sports pavilion, bending to R across green to Weavers Pond. Dismount and walk round edge of green, heading towards village hall, then TL onto B2126, SP Forest Green among others.

√ Halfway through sharp S-bend at Cox Corner TL into Mole Street. Keep SO past Stanton Homestead. Optional TL into no through road SP Okewood Church, otherwise continue past Gatton Manor then TL at TJ into Wallis Wood.

⑤ TR after Scarlett Arms into Froggetts Lane, SP Ewhurst. Just after house called Greylands TR onto BY (Lowerhouse Lane). At far end TR onto road by Lyefield House. At B2127 TR for Forest Green.

The Ride

① Forest Green to Ewhurst Green

Forest Green: By its name and its appearance, Forest Green shows how most of the villages and settlements in this area developed. At one time these heavy clay soils were covered in a thick forest – the Anderida Silva of Roman times, which later became known as the Andresweald by the Saxons. The area was never entirely uninhabited, since the raw materials for smelting iron – wood for charcoal and ironstone – were exploited here long before the Romans came, but it was not until the 13th century that recognisable settlements were created in clearings carved out of the forest. Approach Forest Green from the direction of Ockley and its origins are still obvious.

There isn't a great deal in the hamlet even now. The most obvious building is the Parrot Inn, said to be a 15th century building which originated as a hunting lodge for the Wotton Estate of the Evelyn family. It was described not so long ago as 'lovely and rambling', but unsympathetic refurbishment and the opening out of rooms has destroyed much of its character.

There is also an active forge on the edge of the green, a small church built in 1892 as a memorial to a young man shot accidentally while out rabbiting, and the green itself, with its cricket pitch.

But small as the hamlet may be, it does have a special claim to fame: the carol 'O Little Town of Bethlehem' originated here as a folk song.

The Parrot Inn, Forest Green. Free house. 01306 621339. Open all day. Food G

From Forest Green head west on the B2127 road in the direction of Ewhurst – if you parked outside the church, turn left onto the road. Although this is one of the more important roads in the area, it's not too busy most of the time, but it does wind a lot, a characteristic which has much to do with the nature of the soil. In 1823 Cobbett wrote that the three miles of road between Ewhurst, Forest Green, and Ockley were made of the deepest clay he'd ever seen. It took him a good one and a half hours to do the journey on horseback.

As the road leaves Forest Green it crosses one of the many streams which flow from the hills to the north. It then climbs a short slope, and passes a junction with a minor lane on the right. About 300 yards further on, it bends sharply to the right at the junction with Lyefield Lane (Stubbetts Corner) and then crosses into the parish of Ewhurst. On the right, through the trees, you can see Holmbury Hill.

☞ *To connect with Ride B turn right into Holmbury Hill Road, the second on the right after Stubbetts Corner. Join the route at Radnor Road, near Holmbury House school.*

The road dips sharply after its junction with Plough Lane and soon enters the outskirts of Ewhurst. On the left is a row of unexciting modern houses but open fields opposite help to limit the suburban feel. When you get to the T-junction at the Bulls Head Inn (2 miles), turn left.

☞ *To connect with Ride E in Volume I, turn right here into Shere Road, then fork right after ¾-mile into Peaslake Road.*

Ewhurst, meaning the 'Yew Wood', is described in some books as 'disappointing'. There's some justice in this, but it wasn't always so. When Cobbett passed through in 1823 he thought it 'a very pretty village', and from someone who had no qualms about criticising anything, that was praise indeed. It's not that the village has become ugly, simply that most of its modern buildings are nondescript. The older jewels fight to stand out, but they're swamped.

Ewhurst church

The church is sited on a slight hill in the centre of the village, opposite the village school. It is of Norman origin but was largely rebuilt in the 1830s. That became necessary when workmen who were underpinning the tower made a mistake and it crashed down, taking much of the building with it! A broken gravestone behind the church is a reminder of this calamity. Part of the church and the lychgate are roofed with Horsham stone, an attractive material with which you'll become very familiar on this ride.

The church is set back from the road and is flanked by a group of cottages which set the scene most charmingly. One of the cottages, now called the Old Post Office, was once the Bull Inn. Before he started out on his laborious journey to Ockley, Cobbett called there and treated his horse to some oats and himself to a rasher of bacon. No doubt they were glad of the sustenance by the end of the ride!

▦ *The Bulls Head, The Street. 01483 277447. Free house. Food G Rest Acc*

⎫ *Hazelbank Stores, The Street. 8–5 Mon, 8–5.30 Tue–Fri, 8–1 Sat, 8.30–12 Sun, closed for lunch 1–2.15.*
⎫ *Ewhurst Post Office, The Street. Normal PO hours (closed for lunch).*

At the far end of the village, as the main road to Cranleigh bends to the right, continue straight ahead into Horsham Lane, signposted 'Ellens Green & Horsham'. This leads to Ewhurst Green, which is surrounded by the same mix of attractive older properties and less appealing modern ones as the rest of the village, although it's strangely detached from it. Plough Lane comes in on the left by the phone box halfway across the green.

② Ewhurst Green to Oakwood Hill

Continue along Horsham Lane past the cricket ground (3 miles), opposite which is the aptly-named Square Leg Cottage. About 450 yards further on turn right into Somersbury Lane, signed for 'Ellens Green'. A lovely downhill run follows, past the imposing gates of Coxland, with Somersbury Manor to the left.

The stream which goes under the road at the bottom of the valley, known as Cobbler's Brook, flows past Cranleigh and Bramley (where it's often known as the Bramley Wey), before joining the Wey and thus the Thames. Just a few miles to the east you will cross streams which flow in a different direction – south to the River Arun and so to the Channel.

After crossing the bridge the road rises and soon passes Deepdene Kennels (4 miles). This stretch of road is bordered by a variety of woodland and open fields, a mixture which is typical of the Weald and which persists throughout the ride. There is a small cluster of houses around Nags Wood, and a few hundred yards after that the lane joins the B2128 Cranleigh to Rudgwick road, just by the Old Oast Kennels. Turn left.

The 5-mile point is midway between the junction and Pollingfold Manor. About 250 yards after the Manor is a derelict section of raised footway, showing that the road must once have been prone to flooding by the small stream which passes under it. Just beyond it, on the right, is the Wheatsheaf pub.

🍺 *The Wheatsheaf, Horsham Road, Ellen's Green. King & Barnes. 01403 822155. Open 11–3, 6–11, Sundays 12–3, 7–10.30 Food C G Rest (closed Sunday eves)*

At Ellen's Green, about 400 yards after the pub, turn left into Furzen Lane. There's a phone box on the small green by the junction. Just around the corner is a lovely group of cottages, including the old school, and further along, on the right, is Ellens (6 miles).

Ellens *is a grade II listed mansion which, like so many of Surrey's large houses, has recently been divided into three separate homes, having previously declined into a sorry state. In 1914 the architect Maurice Webb vastly extended a farmhouse built in the 16th or 17th century to create an Elizabethan-style manor house. The front elevation is half-timbered, but the rear, which looks out over the Sussex border, is mainly tile-hung. The formal gardens are said to have been based on those at Hampton Court.*

The lane passes another delightful group of cottages as it leaves Ellen's Green and heads out into the open countryside. Notice how all the fields are edged by thick belts of trees called shaws. They are relics of the time when the law demanded that strips of woodland be retained around each field when the forest was cleared, as timber was a vital resource.

At the T-junction at the end of the lane (7 miles) turn left following the signpost for 'Ewhurst & Oakwood Hill'. At the next junction, a quarter of a mile further on, stay on the same road as it bends to the right for Oakwood Hill.

Several local properties have 'Monks' in their name, but there is no obvious religious significance. Monks Farm is situated some way across the fields. It stands on the course of Stane Street, the old Roman road from London to Chichester, taking advantage of the more solid foundations offered by the road formation than the surrounding clay.

The local 'big house' was known, until recently, simply as Monks but, as with Ellens, property developers have found that adding the suffix 'Manor' appeals to potential buyers.

Further along the road, Monks Tower lives up to its name; it would be a typical Surrey cottage but for the curious three-storey tower, topped by a weathervane, in the middle of its front.

Boswells Farm

The 8-mile point is passed near Pound Farm. Notice how far back the hedges are on this stretch, showing that the lane was once used for driving cattle, the wide verges providing grazing on the journey. As you approach Woodhams Farm the lane widens even further, before it comes to a junction by Okewood Manor. The turning to the left offers a short-cut back to Forest Green, but otherwise continue to the right towards the Punchbowl Inn.

Oakwood Hill delights in uncertainty as to the spelling of its name, which is quite an achievement for such a small place. Okewood Hill and even Oakwoodhill are in common use, and it's no use asking the locals – they all seem to differ. The pub is as close as the hamlet comes to having a centre but the church is half a mile away by footpath through the woods. By road it's nearer two miles! You'll have the option of visiting it at a later stage in the ride.

Parts of the Punchbowl Inn date from the 14th century. Note its massive chimneys, one

of which has recently been built or rebuilt to match the others. A good job has also been made of repairing its Horsham stone roof.

The Punchbowl, Oakwood Hill. Free house (Badger). 01306 627249. Open all day. Food Midday–10pm including Sunday, Coffee and tea, G

③ Oakwood Hill to Ockley

From the pub head downhill past the phone box and then turn right almost immediately into the unsigned Ruckmans Lane. Watch out for the farm track leading to Ruckmans Farm; it follows the line of the Roman Stane Street. Boswells Farm, just along the lane, is used by the Surrey Union hunt. Whatever one's views on this activity, the use of the farmhouse as kennels has preserved it in a pre-20th century state.

Beyond Boswells the lane comes to the main A29 Bognor road (9 miles). Despite the traffic, spare a moment to admire the view to the left towards Leith Hill, then cross over and continue along the lane – Paynes Green Road – on the far side.

The next stage of the route is possibly the most delightful part of the ride. Paynes Green Road (and Weare Street, which it soon becomes) is a narrow lane, winding through some marvellous countryside.

Paynes Green is no more than a small roadside huddle of cottages which isn't enhanced by the premises of a wine shipping company. Beyond it the lane bends to cross a bridge over the North River, a tributary of the River Arun.

Smugglers Lane: *The bridleway on the right after the bridge is one of many tracks in these parts which rejoice in the name of Smugglers Lane. The neighbourhood was a favourite with smugglers because the hills to the north provided an ideal halfway house between the coast and London, where goods could be discreetly tucked away. Horsham, not far to the south, was a major smuggling centre.*

The quiet lanes through this difficult countryside may well have offered the smugglers well-hidden routes for their trains of packhorses, but myths and legends about their activities have grown over the years so that the real story is obscured. Smuggling is usually thought of as a furtive activity but, in many cases, rather than risk getting stuck in poorly-maintained lanes and tracks, huge well-armed gangs simply carried their goods along the main roads. Their numbers and fearsome reputation deterred interference!

Weare Street's Gill Cottage (10 miles), on the right, is tucked almost below the level of road. Its name is appropriate; there is a deep gill beside the road, carved by a tributary of the North River. The lane now enters a wooded area, part of it showing signs of coppicing in times gone by; this involved trees being cut down to their stumps so that new shoots would grow to

provide a crop of poles. The coppice here has not been harvested and the poles are now substantial trunks.

Beside the entrance to Holbrook Farm (11 miles) is a covered stand which used to hold milk churns awaiting collection. There is also a small pond with a surprising number of ducks, moorhens and other water birds. You are now faced by a gentle uphill climb and you may hear trains passing close by. The tracks themselves are not obvious, but if you look beside Sherwood Cottage you'll see the gates where a bridleway crosses them.

☞ *To link with Ride D follow this bridleway, which passes through Grenehurst Park to come out on the A24 at Clark's Green roundabout.*

☞ *There are two ways of reaching Ockley from this point. The more pleasant and interesting is the bridleway route past Vann Lake, but this may not be suitable after wet weather. The alternative route by road is described on page 32.*

Turn left into the entrance of Stylehurst Farm, just after the bend by Sherwood Cottage. The bridleway sign has been turned round but it should point along the tarred drive, called Vann Lake Road. Go along the drive past a mobile home park and when it divides (a sign lists the houses served by each branch), go straight ahead (ie take the left branch).

The tarred drive ends by the penultimate house (12 miles) but the track which continues past the Vann Lake Nature Reserve is in reasonable condition. You can just see the lake in the bottom of the valley through the trees. It is artificial, and was probably built around the time Vann House was rebuilt in 1850.

If you want a closer view of the lake and the nature reserve – which is owned by the Surrey Wildlife Trust and well worth visiting – you must walk down the narrow, signposted footpath which branches off a little further along on the right and crosses over the spillway.

The bridleway eventually becomes a narrow path, unsurfaced but with occasional patches repaired with hard-core, but within a short distance it comes to a junction with another bridleway. Turn right here and go down the slope. At the bottom cross the bridge over the stream (which is fed by Vann Lake) and climb the short, sharp slope on the other side.

The track divides at the top – take the path between the cast iron gateposts on the right. The first stretch is surfaced with old road works chippings but the rest is clay and grass, which is bumpy in dry weather and could give problems after heavy rain. The path heads towards Vann House but curves away to the left before reaching it, emerging between ornamental gateposts by the gate of Vann Croft Cottage.

Take the tarred drive opposite the gates of Vann House (not the one which leads to Vann Farm) and follow it out on to a lane called Friday Street. Pass a small group of cottages and continue to the end of the lane where it joins the A29 at Ockley (13 miles).

There are several pubs and a couple of shops in Ockley; the Cricketers Arms and the garage (with its shop) are to the left of the junction, but all the other facilities are to the right.

You can turn right onto the A29 if you wish, but the road is busy. The better route is across the green, not least because it gives a closer view of the many superb houses and cottages which line it, so cross the A29 to the gravelled track opposite. Pass the sports pavilion and follow the track which bends to the right across the green. Dismount at Weavers Pond, where the track ends, and walk your bike round the edge of the green.

Vann Lake

From here you can see how the main road, the old Roman Stane Street, was built on a ledge along the gently sloping hillside above the green. At one time the road was lined with elms, and a most attractive avenue they must have made. The village well is in the middle of the green; the machinery has gone and the impressive structure which covered it shelters nothing more than a bench.

Ockley: *Ask any villager about the history of the place and you will surely be told this was the site of the Battle of Aclea when the Saxons of Wessex fought off the invading Danes in the year 851. Historians have their doubts – there were several places called Aclea – but you'll find few locals who share them.*

The Anglo-Saxon Chronicle, written more than 1,000 years ago, tells us how the Danes landed on the Kent coast and quickly defeated Athelstan, the under-king who ruled Kent, Sussex, Essex and Surrey. Having sacked Canterbury, the Danes marched on London, where they also defeated Beorhtwulf, king of Mercia. Then, flushed with success, they turned their attention on Winchester, capital of Wessex.

Ethelwulf, king of Wessex (and father of Alfred the Great), responded to the threat by marching north, along Stane Street it is said, and blocking the Danes' path.

Tradition says the confrontation took place on Ockley Green itself, but it has been suggested that if the battle did indeed take place here, it would surely have been fought on the higher and drier ground below Leith Hill. What's known for certain is that the Danes were heavily defeated. 'Blood stood ankle deep' according to the record, and by the evening not a Dane remained alive on the battlefield to bury their dead.

Ockley is unusual in having two churches. The parish church is some way from the centre of population, so a small one was built in the corner of the green, by the school, in the late 19th century. The parish church itself is near Ockley Court, on the road to Capel. Although it dates from the 13th century (the tower was added in 1699), it was rebuilt in 1873. John Aubrey, the 17th century antiquarian, recorded the Ockley tradition of planting red rose trees on the graves of betrothed lovers who died before they married.

Ockley has a marvellous selection of listed buildings, especially around the green. Carpoles Cottages, named after the carp ponds which were once situated nearby, and Tanyard Cottages are worth a special look. Their builders didn't plan them to look so wonderful but succeeded, whereas we try so hard to achieve the same effect and usually fail!

🍴 *The Cricketers Arms, Stane Street. Free house. 01306 627205.*
🍴 *The Old School House, Stane Street. King & Barnes. 01306 627430. Food C Rest*
🍴 *The King's Arms, Stane Street. Free house. 01306 711224 Food Rest Acc*
🍴 *The Red Lion, Stane Street. 01306 711032. Open all day Food C Rest*
🛒 *The Old Bakery and Post Office*

As you head towards the far end of the green you may find it easier to cut across to the road junction opposite the village hall. From there, turn left onto the B2126.

√ Ockley to Wallis Wood

As the B2126 leaves Ockley it passes Jayes Park on the left and, after crossing the recently-rebuilt Hatch Pond Bridge, there is a sharp climb. The road appears to be heading straight towards the hills but, at the last moment, bends sharply away to the left (14 miles). Leith Hill is little more than a mile away and the tower on its summit, almost 1,000 feet above sea level, stands out clearly.

Halfway through the sharp S-bend at Cox Corner, turn left into Mole Street, another splendid, deserted country lane.

☞ *To connect with Ride C continue for a short distance past the junction with Mole Street and turn right into Leith Hill Lane.*

A short distance along Mole Street is the entrance to Gosterwood Manor Farm, which marks the ride's 15-mile point. Keep straight on, ignoring both the unmarked turning on the right at Castle Cottage and the later turning on the left signposted to 'Ockley' (16 miles).

Mole Street becomes Standon Lane at this second junction. It passes the entrance to Standon Homestead, with its milk churn stand, and then winds before dipping to cross the Standon Brook by a small bridge.

There is a sharp rise up the other side to a junction with a 'no through road' signposted 'Okewood Church'. Follow this sign along a somewhat pot-holed lane past some scattered houses and cottages until you come to the dead-end at the church (17 miles).

Okewood Church, *dedicated to St John the Baptist, has been described as one of the loneliest in Surrey, and when you see it you'll surely find that claim hard to dispute. The church sits amid the trees, and is approached from the road by a path which crosses a woodland stream on a small timber bridge.*

It was founded in the 13th century as a forest chapel to save local people a long walk or ride to the far-off parish church. It was restored and enlarged in the 15th century thanks to the lucky outcome of an accident. Sir Edward de la Hale was hunting wild boar in the forest with his son when the boy was thrown from his horse and charged by a wounded boar. There was nothing his father could do, but suddenly an arrow flew through the trees and killed the boar outright. In gratitude for his son's life having been spared Sir Edward paid for the chapel to be restored.

In 1853 the church gained its own vicar (it now shares one with Ockley and Forest Green), and later that century it was enlarged and again restored. Electric lighting wasn't laid on until the 1960s – even so, the chandeliers still use candles and each pew has its pair of candleholders. On the south wall some wall paintings survive. Take a look up into the gallery as well, and spot the carved face looking down at the bell-ringer. At one time there were two of them on opposite sides.

On leaving the church, return along Church Lane until you come to the road again, and turn left to continue on your way. The road is signposted to the Gatton Manor Golf & Country Club and passes the Hannah Peschar Gallery on the way.

Hannah Peschar Gallery and Sculpture Garden, *at Black and White Cottage, Standon Lane, Ockley, is described as an exhibition of sculpture and ceramics in an exotic and dramatic watergarden designed by Anthony Paul. Open second Sun in May to 31st October. Fri and Sat 11-6, Sun and BHs 2-5, Tue to Thur by appointment only (buyers and group visits). Closed Mon. £4 adult, £3 child, £2 concession.* ☎ *01306 627269*

A steady uphill climb follows, past the entrance to Gatton Manor, after which there is a sharp left-hand bend at a junction with a no through road.

At the end of the lane (18 miles) turn left into the hamlet of Wallis Wood, which has a small green with a covered well like the one at Ockley, but here the machinery is still in place. The 17th century Scarlett Arms pub is opposite the school. Notice the difference in the spelling of the pub's name between the sign and the front wall!

🍺 *The Scarlett Arms, Wallis Wood. King & Barnes. 01306 627243. Food G*

⑤ Wallis Wood to Forest Green

Turn right almost immediately after the Scarlett Arms into Froggetts Lane. The lane, which is signposted 'Ewhurst', twists past Wallis Wood Farm and Froggetts. Just after a house called Greylands, turn right onto a public byway. There's an awkward patch of gravel at the start but, other than

The Scarlett Arms, Wallis Wood

this, the byway has been repaired to a very high standard. As the tyre tracks show, it can be used by vehicles, so keep a look out.

Called Lowerhouse Lane, this was once part of the turnpike from Abinger through Pitland Street (Holmbury) to Wallis Wood which was built in the late 18th century.

At the end of the byway turn right onto the road by Lyefield House. After a short distance it begins to climb steeply (20 miles) and passes East Breache.

Just beyond Cobbets Farm and Cobbetts House, an attractive building with a timber frame and brick infill, turn right onto the B2127 Forest Green–Ewhurst road, and follow it back to Forest Green and the end of the ride (21½ miles by the church).

Alternative section of route

③ Oakwood Hill to Ockley

☞ *This alternative bypasses the bridleway route via Vann Lake.*

Continue along Weare Street to the T-junction with the B2126 Capel–Forest Green road. (⇌ Ockley station is a short way to the right.) Turn left and follow the road past Ockley Court and the village church. The church is beautiful but the red brick of the surrounding walls and buildings can be oppressive, although in summer the effect is relieved by a fantastic display of flowering baskets and tubs.

After a few hundred yards the road comes to the A29. Turn left, taking care because of the traffic, pass the King's Arms and then turn right into Lake Road.

Ride B:
Hidden in the Hills

Broadmoor Hill • Leylands • Abinger Bottom • Pasture Wood • Holmbury St
Mary • Holmbury Hill • Radnor Road • Peaslake • Hoe • Sutton Abinger •
Abinger • Friday Street • Broadmoor Hill

Distance: 10¾ miles
Landranger Maps: 187
Pathfinder Maps: 1226

While Box Hill and Leith Hill often swarm with tourists, the lanes and woods
around Holmbury are almost always peaceful. A few places in the area –
notably the comfortable pubs – attract visitors, but not in overwhelming
numbers. Much of the time you'll find yourself alone in the hidden beauty of
these hills.

There are some climbs on this ride, but not as many as you might think, and
the views and the scenery make them worthwhile. Unusually for our rides,
this one sticks almost entirely to surfaced roads and lanes, making it less
strenuous than others. Most of these lanes are so quiet there is no need to
resort to off-road tracks to escape the traffic.

You could quite well make this a half-day ride but, with so much beautiful
scenery along the way, it's not really one to be rushed. If you can, take a pair
of binoculars and be prepared to sit a while to make the most of some superb
views.

Starting Points

Start at the Broadmoor Hill car park (grid
reference TQ 132455) on Sheephouse
Lane, Wotton – the turning off the A25
Guildford–Dorking road beside the Wotton
Hatch pub. There is also a car park on the
outskirts of Friday Street, one on Radnor
Road (near Holmbury Hill), and another
in Pond Lane, Peaslake. All are free, and all
except the one in Peaslake have ample
space.

⇌ Access to this ride by rail isn't too
easy. The nearest station is at Gomshall on
the Guildford–Dorking–Redhill line
(Thames Trains), but most of the time it

has only one train every two hours. From
Gomshall station head east along the A25
to the green at Abinger Hammer and then
turn right onto the B2126 towards
Holmbury St Mary. Sutton Abinger, where
you join the ride, is about a mile along it.

Note: Ride C also begins at the car park at
Broadmoor Hill and the two rides can be
linked at this point.

Ride B
Hidden in the Hills

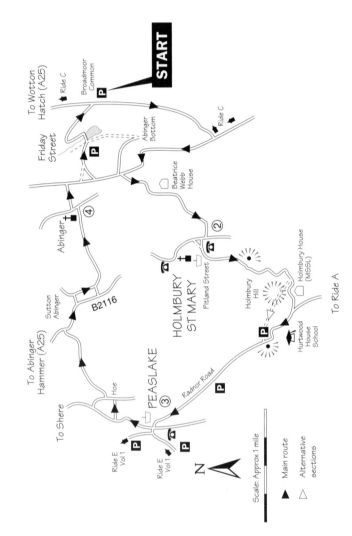

START

To Wotton
Hatch (A25)

◄ Ride C

Broadmoor
Common

Ride C

Friday
Street

Abinger
Bottom

Beatrice
Webb
House

Abinger

④

Sutton
Abinger

B2116

To Abinger
Hammer (A25)

HOLMBURY
ST MARY

Pitland Street

Holmbury
Hill

Holmbury House
(MSSL)

To Ride A

Hurtwood
House
School

To Shere

Hoe

PEASLAKE

③

Radnor Road

Ride E
Vol 1

Ride E
Vol 1

N

Scale: Approx 1 mile

▲ Main route

△ Alternative
sections

The Route in Brief

① TL out of CP. At TJ with Leith Hill Road, TR, SP Abinger Common & Wotton. About 350 yds after Z-bend TL into Pasture Wood Road. At TJ with the B2126 Horsham Road TR then immediately L into Pitland Street, SP Peaslake.

② Go SO along Holmbury Hill Road (continuation of Pitland Street), curving around Holmbury Hill. At next TJ TR into Radnor Road, SP Peaslake. Pass Hurtwood Control car parks 1 and 11 and continue to Peaslake.

③ TR into Peaslake Lane (which becomes Pursers Lane) then take 2nd on R, Hoe Lane. Follow road to left at junc with Franks Field, then TR into continuation of Hoe Lane. At TJ with B2126 TR, then take next L, Raikes Lane, SP Abinger Common & Leith Hill.

Immediately before Volunteer pub TR into Water Lane, also SP Abinger Common & Leith Hill. Follow road to left at next junc, where it becomes Sutton Lane. At next TJ TL towards church and pub.

√ Immediately before pub TR into narrow lane, Donkey Lane. At next junc TR. Either take next BW on left, or continue to next junc and TL, SP Friday Street. Cross dam and climb hill on far side. At top TR, SP Leith Hill. CP is 200 yds on L.

A quiet lane near Friday Street

The Ride

① Broadmoor Hill to Holmbury St Mary

Turn left as you leave the car park at Broadmoor Hill, from where the narrow lane climbs gently through woodland, passing Leylands (once the home of Arthur Brooke, son of the founder of the Brooke Bond tea company), Wotton Barn, and Leylands Farm. Beyond them, there is open common on both sides of the road.

Tucked away on the right, reached by a track off the road, is the Old Observatory (1 mile), now the home of the County Council's countryside ranger but once an outpost of the Royal Observatory at Greenwich. Between 1940 and 1955 it was the source of the Greenwich time signal 'pips'.

Continue to the T-junction with Leith Hill Road and then turn right in the direction of Abinger Common and Wotton. After a long downhill run through the woods, the road curves sharply to the left and then, a few moments later, more gently to the right (2 miles). At the junction about 350 yards after this bend, take the small turning on the left – Pasture Wood Road – which leads to the village of Holmbury.

☞ *Before turning off, you may like to explore the small lane on the right which leads down a steep hill to the delightful hamlet of Abinger Bottom. Follow the lane until you come to Spring Cottage, beyond which is a small pool fed by a spring – the round trip is just over a mile.*

Returning to the main route, Pasture Wood Road passes the entrance to Beatrice Webb House, for many years after World War II a Labour Party education centre, named after the prominent socialist economist. The house, originally called

Pasture Wood House, has gardens designed by the famous Surrey gardener Gertrude Jekyll, and was extended by Lutyens.

The entrance to Belmont Preparatory School is followed by a 1 in 8 downhill slope through woodland. At the bottom (3 miles) there is a clearing, and then the road climbs up past Pasture Wood Cottage and Bulmer Farm (B&B), both on the right, before descending again to a junction with the B2126 Horsham Road by the entrance to Hopedene. This is Holmbury St Mary. Turn right and then immediately left into Pitland Street, in the direction of Peaslake.

Holmbury St Mary didn't exist until Victorian times. Before that there were two small hamlets, Pitland Street and Felday, which still form recognisably-separate places, each with its own pub. Amazingly, there are also the remains of twin settlements from much earlier times. It has long been known that there was an Iron Age hill-fort on the top of Holmbury Hill, but it was only in the 1980s that another enclosure of similar date but much larger size was discovered on the ridge above Felday. The two may have performed different roles, the one at Felday being an enclosure for animals.

The focus of the Victorian village was provided by St Mary's church, which stands above the green at the Felday end. Designed by G E Street, the architect of the Royal Courts of Justice in London, and built at his own expense, it was completed in 1879. Street and his first wife loved the area, and he designed the house Holmdale for them to move into. Sadly, Mrs Street died before it was finished in 1873.

Holmbury boasts the first purpose-built youth hostel in England. It's still in use, providing cheap accommodation for those wanting to explore the surrounding country.

🏠 *Royal Oak, The Green (near the church). Free house. 01306 730120. Food 12.30– 2.30, 6.30–9.30 C G Acc*

St Mary's church, Holmbury

🏠 *King's Head, Pitland Street. Free house.
Food G*
🛒 *Village Stores, 9–6 (Mon 9–1, Sat & Sun
9–4)*

☞ *The route of the ride passes through
Pitland Street. To visit Felday and the
church, turn right along the Horsham Road.*

② Holmbury St Mary to Peaslake

Pitland Street climbs steeply away from
the Horsham Road. The King's Head pub
and the village shop can be found along a
turning on the right.

The ride continues past the Coach House,
where Pitland Street becomes Holmbury
Hill Road. Fortunately, the lane hugs the
side of the hill and no serious climbing is
involved. From near the house called
Moxley (4 miles) there are some good

views to the east across the valley towards
Leith Hill, as well as over the Weald to the
south, though you may have to peer
through gaps in the roadside bushes to see
them. The prospect is more open a little
further on.

Several large Victorian houses line the
road. They were built for wealthy London
businessmen, attracted to the area by the
opening, in 1849, of the Redhill–
Guildford railway, which enabled them to
reach their offices in the City with ease.

At one point the road appears to head
straight for the gateway of Holmbury
House, one of these large mansions. It was
built in about 1860 and about ten years
later it became the property of the Hon.
Frederick Leveson-Gower. William
Gladstone, then Prime Minister, was a
regular visitor and it is said the entire
Cabinet went there on one occasion. It's

Peaslake

now used by the Mullard Space Science Laboratory (MSSL), part of University College, London.

The road continues on the right-hand side of the gateway, climbing sharply for a short distance, before reaching a level stretch past some cottages which nestle into the side of Holmbury Hill. The 857-feet high summit, with its Iron Age hill-fort, is immediately to the right.

A bridleway heads to the right just before the cottages. If you don't mind a very steep climb, it offers an interesting alternative route, passing over the top of the hill and through the fort, before rejoining the main route at car park 1.

A little further on, a recently-renewed brick wall borders the grounds of Ariel House, another part of the MSSL. Rhododendrons thrive on the acid, sandy soil, and during May and June they provide a

spectacle of roadside colour. A brief downhill run ends at a T-junction.

☞ *Turn left at this junction to link with Ride A on the Ewhurst–Forest Green road.*

Turn right into Radnor Road in the direction signed 'Peaslake' and begin a substantial climb. The large house to the left is Hurtwood House, now a private school and at the top of the hill (just over 5 miles) is Hurtwood Control car park 1.

The view from the road is good, but that from the car park, at a slightly greater height, is tremendous. Having rounded Holmbury Hill, the vista is now to the west. Immediately in front of you is Pitch Hill, with the Duke of Kent School (see Ride E in volume 1) nestling beneath it, while beyond it can be seen Hascombe Hill, several miles away. Looking behind you on a clear day, you can see the South Downs in the far distance. The road now heads downhill through woods. Hurtwood Control car park 11 is just before the 6-mile point and Peaslake village is about half a mile beyond that.

Peaslake lies at the heart of the Hurtwood, the largest area of common land in Surrey, amounting to over 4,000 acres of the Greensand hills south of the A25 Guildford–Dorking road. Although the village has existed as such for only the past 100 years, it's a thriving community, with a substantial hotel, a busy village shop, and a determined campaign to re-open its village school.

⌗ ☕ *The Hurtwood Inn, Walking Bottom. Free house. 01306 730851. Open all day. Food C G Rest Acc, also morning coffee and afternoon teas.*

🛒 *Peaslake Village Stores & PO. Open 8–8 (Sun 9–8)*

📖 *At Peaslake you can link with Ride E in Volume 1, West Surrey.*

③ Peaslake to Abinger

Turn right past the Village Stores into Peaslake Lane (which becomes Pursers Lane) and follow it to the junction with Hoe Lane, opposite some derelict green-houses (7 miles). Turn right here and climb the sharp slope past Hoe Farm. At the top follow the road as it bends to the left at its junction with Franks Field, then turn right opposite a row of cottages into the continuation of Hoe Lane.

A steep descent into a dip is followed by a climb – almost as steep – to a small crossroads, and then another downhill run. This ends at the junction with the B2126 Horsham Road, opposite Little Brook. Turn right here.

The road can be busy, so take care, but fortunately you soon turn off. About 350 yards beyond the entrance to Sutton Place (8 miles) turn left into Raikes Lane,

Sutton Abinger

Banned!

signposted 'Abinger Common & Leith Hill'. There's a wonderful cluster of cottages around this junction and it's well worth pausing for a few moments to enjoy them. The Volunteer Inn is just ahead; note the sundial on its front wall – it's obviously a modern version, since it's lit up at night by an electric light!

📖 *The Volunteer, Raikes Lane, Sutton Abinger. Friary Meux. 01306 730798. Food (12–2, 7–9, 7 days a week) G Rest Acc*

Immediately before the pub turn right into Water Lane, which is also signposted 'Abinger Common & Leith Hill'. Pass the entrance to Frolbury Manor, and bear round to the left at the next junction, where the road becomes Sutton Lane. A long, steady climb follows, passing the gates of Abinger Manor (9 miles). At the next junction turn left towards the church and the Abinger Hatch pub. The route turns right into the small lane just before the pub, but don't be in too much of a hurry to move on.

Abinger *claims to be the site of the oldest known dwelling in England, the remains of*

what is said to be a Mesolithic (Stone Age) pit dwelling having been excavated there. The experts are not convinced that it dates from such an early period and some of them doubt whether it was even a dwelling.

Signs of some of the later occupants of the village can be found in the grounds of the manor house, in the form of the motte (or mound) of a Norman castle. However, anyone looking for a stone keep and battlements will be sorely disappointed. The only structures this castle ever had were a palisade, a watchtower, and a bridge, all built of wood, and long since gone.

St James's church may have a look of great antiquity, but little of the original remains, thanks to the misfortunes which have befallen it this century. It was badly damaged when a flying bomb exploded nearby in 1944, and was rebuilt in 1951. Then, in 1964, a lightning strike inflicted yet more damage.

The name of Abinger's inn derives from the old word 'hatch' meaning gate – in this case onto the common. It once drew its water supply from a well no less than 137 feet deep. Instead of a single bucket it had two, used alternately, so that while one was raised the other was at water level.

📖 *The Abinger Hatch, Abinger Lane. Free house. 01306 730737. Food*

③ Abinger to Broadmoor Hill

Coming from Sutton Abinger, turn right into Donkey Lane, the tiny road immediately before you reach the pub. Hidden in the hedge on the left at the entrance to the lane is an old cast-iron notice prohibiting locomotives, motor tractors, heavy motor cars, and motor cars with seats for more than 15 persons! Such signs were commonplace only 20 years ago but very few remain today. Also, note the hoist on the building at the start of the lane; it was once used to lift goods from wagons parked below.

The lane curves downhill, passing the Old Rectory at the bottom, before climbing

Friday Street

sharply to a junction with Hollow Lane. Turn right, climbing the hill past the posts marking the old manor gates. A bridleway branches off to the left just after this point. You can either follow this (when it forks you'll find that the left-hand branch is in better condition but both lead to the same place) or you can continue up the hill to the next road junction and then turn left.

The bridleway rejoins the road at the bottom of the dip, from where there is a brief climb to the Friday Street car park (10 miles), discreetly hidden in the woods on the edge of the hamlet. A final downhill run brings you to Friday Street itself.

Friday Street *is remarkable in having survived, untouched, as nothing more than a few houses and a pub clustered on the edge of a pool, framed by pine-clad hillsides. Its beauty stems as much from its tranquillity as its setting, and long may this remain unchanged.*

The pool, formed by damming a tributary of the Tillingbourne, was probably built as a hammer pond to drive an early ironworks, and, if that's so, it's one of the few in Surrey to survive intact. It was subsequently used to drive a corn mill.

Below the dam the stream flows through the private grounds of the Wotton Estate, where it has been landscaped into a series of fishponds and weirs. A delightful footpath, which can be reached from the lane by the postbox at the end of the dam, follows the stream all the way to Wotton House and is well worth exploring, but on foot rather than your bike.

The Stephan Langton pub is along the lane leading to the right by the side of the pool. It is named after the 13th century Archbishop of Canterbury who joined with the barons to force King John to sign the Magna Carta. Tradition has it that Langton was born in Friday Street but, unfortunately, this is just another of those charming Surrey legends which sprang from fertile and romantic imaginations in the Victorian age, in this case the local historian Martin Tupper.

The Stephan Langton. Free house. 01306 730775. Food (not Mon eves) Patio Rest

From the hamlet, cross the dam and follow the narrow, winding lane as it climbs very steeply through the woods. When you reach the junction at the top, turn right in the direction signposted 'Leith Hill'.

To join Ride C, turn left at this junction.

Broadmoor Hill car park, and the end of the ride, is about 200 yards from the junction on the left.

Ride C:
The Surrey Mountaineer

Broadmoor Hill • Wotton • The Rookery • Westcott • Logmore • Robbing Gate
• Coldharbour • Leith Hill • Wotton Common • Broadmoor Hill

Distance: 10½ miles
Landranger Maps: 187
Pathfinder Maps: 1226

Does Surrey have a mountain? It does, if you accept that a hill of more than 1,000 feet qualifies for that title. In that case, Leith Hill, the highest point in south-east England, just makes it, provided you include the tower on its summit. Whether it really justifies being called a mountain or not, the scenery is certainly spectacular. In late Victorian times the area became known as Little Switzerland, for obvious reasons.

Don't let the idea of endless hill-climbing put you off this ride, though. There is some, to be sure, but far less than you might imagine, and a bike is certainly the best way to enjoy the magnificent scenery. You can stop wherever and whenever you like, which you cannot with a car on these narrow lanes, and in a car you can't afford to take your eyes off the road.

The superb scenery isn't limited to the highest parts of this ride though. It passes through some delightful spots nestling in the valleys of the Tillingbourne and Pippbrook streams, some of them tranquil and little known despite being only yards from the bustling A25.

Some parts of the tracks at the beginning of the ride may be muddy or rough, but they are worth persevering with because of the delightful route they follow.

Starting Points

Start at the Broadmoor Hill car park on Sheephouse Lane, Wotton (grid reference TQ 132455). Sheephouse Lane joins the A25 Guildford–Dorking road immediately beside the Wotton Hatch pub. There are also a number of car parks around the foot of Leith Hill, but remember that you'll end the ride with an uphill climb if you start from one of these.

≥ The nearest stations are in Dorking, a couple of miles along the A25 from Westcott. Dorking station is served by frequent trains from Waterloo (South West Trains) and Victoria (Connex South Central), via Epsom and Leatherhead.

Dorking West and Dorking Deepdene stations are on the Guildford–Dorking–Redhill line operated by Thames Trains. (Dorking West is the nearest of all the stations to Westcott, but its services are more limited than those to the other stations.)

Ride C
The Surrey Mountaineer

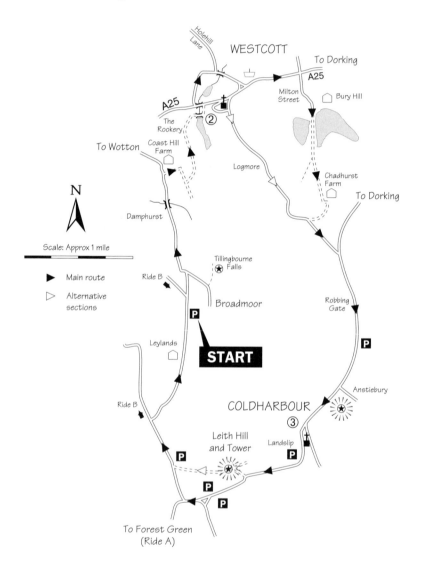

The Route in Brief

① TR out of CP then SO at turnings to Friday Street and Broadmoor. Just before Coast Hill Farm TR onto BY (red waymark arrow). (BY is paralleled by FP behind hedge.)

After 200 yards BY bends R, and divides immediately afterwards – take L fork (red arrow marks route). After another 200 yards THL onto rough BW which almost turns back the way you have come and goes steeply downhill. Continue SO until it joins driveway of The Rookery. Follow this to junction with A25.

② TL onto A25 (CAUTION busy road) then immediately R into Balchins Lane. This becomes Westcott Street at bridge. Holehill Lane (on L) offers pleasant diversion (see text). SO along Westcott Street to junction with A25.

③ TL onto A25 for almost half a mile, then TR into Milton Street. After last cottage, lane becomes narrow BW between lakes of Bury Hill Fisheries. Keep SO to gate into grassy field. Through gate and follow BW diagonally across field towards lone oak tree. Leave field through gate onto track to Chadhurst Farm.

At farm veer slightly L (keep L of building with timber supports) and follow track (BW) uphill. At end TL into Logmore Lane. At TJ TR into Coldharbour Lane. Keep SO to Coldharbour.

√ Through village and SO at next junction, SP 'Leith Hill'. SO at junction after church. (Shortest access to Tower is from bend by Cockshot Farm.) At next junction take R fork, SP 'Abinger Common & Wotton'. After 100 yards TR at next junction, taking uphill road. Just after High Ashes Farm TR, SP 'Broadmoor'. SO to Broadmoor Hill CP.

The Ride

① Broadmoor Hill to The Rookery

Turn right out of the car park and continue past the turnings to Friday Street and Broadmoor, following the signs for Wotton. (By all means try the dead-end lane to Broadmoor if you wish – it's a charming little hamlet in the midst of the woods – but be prepared for the steep climb back up. Look out on the left as you descend the hill to see the Tillingbourne Falls on the far side of the valley.)

After about half a mile there is a cleared area on the right, where young conifers have been planted. This gives a good view across the valley of the infant Tillingbourne stream. The land here is

Tillingbourne Falls

part of the extensive Wotton Estate, which is heavily forested with firs and pine trees. It was one of the first places in the country where Scots Pines were introduced, back in the 18th century.

This part of the journey is mostly downhill through woodland, with the occasional climb to break your headlong dash. Odd breaks in the tree cover are a reminder of the damage suffered in the Great Storm of 1987. Such storms, and their effects, are not uncommon hereabouts. John Evelyn (see panel opposite) wrote of one which blew down 2,000 trees in November 1703.

In places the road runs through deep cuttings in the sandstone, the sides carved by the wind and rain into fantastic, almost primeval shapes. A dip into the valley of the Tillingbourne at Damphurst (1 mile) is followed by a sharp 300-yard climb. About half a mile away to the left is Wotton House, though it cannot be seen from here.

About 100 yards after the top of the climb, turn right onto a track (a byway), just before the buildings of Coast Hill Farm. The track can be very muddy after wet weather and you may prefer to push your bike along the parallel footpath.

After 200 yards the track bends sharply to the right and then forks. Take the left-hand branch, not the track along the edge of the field. A red arrow on a post shows the way.

After a further 200 yards you'll come to another junction of paths. Turn sharp left, almost doubling back on the way you have come, and head steeply down through the trees. It's a rough track and you may need to dismount until you reach the end of the woods, where the path levels out and runs on a ledge along the hillside, giving superb views along the Pippbrook valley towards the Downs.

WOTTON CHURCH.

Wotton House

Wotton House was the family home of the Evelyns, of whom John, the diarist, is the best known. He was born there in 1620 and inherited the estate in 1699 on the death of his brother. His 'Diary' was never intended for publication, but the manuscript was discovered in the library at Wotton by William Bray of Shere (see volume 1), and published by him in 1814. Many people compare it favourably with the more famous Pepys Diaries of the same period. The manuscript is now in Christchurch College, Oxford.

Evelyn was also a landscape designer and tree enthusiast. The terraced gardens he created at Wotton are largely intact, and the surrounding tree-covered hills owe much to him – it's said he introduced the Scots Pine to the area. He also designed the gardens at Albury, including terraces a quarter of a mile long, a tunnel through a hill, a canal, an arcade of yews, and a magnificent holly hedge, but they have not survived so well. He wrote the book 'Sylva', a study of forestry practice, as a result of the indiscriminate felling of trees after the Civil War. The name of Sylvanus Wood, through which the ride passes, commemorates this work, and the estate still boasts a remarkable variety of trees. John Evelyn died in 1705 at the age of 85 and is buried in Wotton Church, just across the A25 (see illustration).

The Evelyn family lived at Wotton until World War II, when it was taken over by the army, afterwards becoming a training college for the fire service. After a period in the ownership of British Telecom, there are now plans to convert it into a conference centre. The building is a jumble of features from different periods from Tudor times to the 19th century. Like the estate, it is private property, although a couple of footpaths pass through the grounds close to it.

Rookery Drive

The ridge you have just crossed is a watershed. To the west the Tillingbourne flows to join the Wey at Shalford, near Guildford, while the Pippbrook runs east to Dorking, where it joins the Mole. Autumn is a splendid time to enjoy this part of the ride, when the trees provide a blaze of golden colours as a backdrop to the view.

In the bottom of the valley, surrounded by trees, are two lakes, once millponds. As you pass the remains of an old gate (2 miles) you'll see some modern houses to the left. They are built on the site of The Rookery, the house where the economist T R Malthus was born in 1766. In his controversial *Essay on the Principle of Population*, published in 1798, he suggested that the population tended to increase faster than the means of subsistence, and therefore sexual restraint needed to be exercised. For this he became known as 'Population Malthus'.

There is a muddy patch before the track leads out onto the drive by the entrance to The Rookery. Turn right, watching for the speed bump. Head along the drive past the delightful cottage called Springs and the equally charming Mill House opposite, beside which the Pippbrook cascades from the lake. (This was one of no fewer than six mills which were once powered by this stream in its short length.) Cross the bridge over the stream and follow the drive round to the left, passing the entrance to Rookery Hill Farm on the right. Be sure to pause by the barn and look back in the direction from which you've come. It's a truly magnificent view.

② The Rookery to Westcott

At the end of the drive, turn left onto the A25 Guildford–Dorking road. Cross the bridge and turn right into Balchins Lane, taking care because of the traffic. Immediately on the left after the turn is the

T-shaped Churtgate House, one part of which is stone-built, the other brick. It's hidden away, but worth a glimpse.

Follow the lane throughout, passing Rookery Farm and the junction with the bridleway to Coombe Farm. The Old Mill House is on the right just before the bridge, where Balchins Lane becomes Westcott Street.

Holehill Lane, a no-through-lane on the left, leads to National Trust land. Walkers are allowed to use the farmtrack through the sheep-fields at the foot of the Downs as a rural route to Dorking via Landbarn Farm. Locals seem to use it as a cycleway, too. (Even if you're not heading for Dorking, the first part of Holehill Lane makes a pleasant diversion off the main route, and is a good spot for picking hazelnuts.)

As you continue along Westcott Street, look along Springfield Road (on the left)

towards the top of the downs and you can see the spire of Ranmore Church (see Ride G). The Old Barracks on the right (3 miles) is a 17th century house of brick with sandstone infill, and a Horsham stone roof. The origin of its name is a mystery, though it may have been a barracks or hostel for estate workers. The junction with the A25 is a short distance further on. The local shops and some of the pubs are just to the left.

Westcott's small green has survived years of thundering traffic on the A25 along its southern edge, and still manages to be one of the most attractive spots on this busy road. The thatched dovecot and the matching bus shelter were built in 1920 to commemorate the end of World War I. They were given by a local resident who lost a son in that conflict.

The village didn't have a church until 1852. Designed by Sir George Gilbert Scott, it's been said that its interior is not one of his best works. The lychgate was added in 1890.

Westcott

🍺 Prince of Wales, Guildford Road. Fullers.
01306 889699. Food G

🍺 Crown Inn, Guildford Road. 01306
885414. Food G

🍺 The Cricketers, Westcott Heath. Free
house. 01306 883520. Food

🛒 Westcott Bakery 7.30–3.30 (2.30 Sats),
closed Sun

🛒 Westcott Newsagency 6.30–6.30 M–F,
7–7 Sat, 7.30–2 Sun

🛒 Balchins Stores 8.30–7 M–Sat, 9–1 Sun

🚲 Nirvana Cycles, Guildford Road. 01306
740300. Sales, hire, & repairs, 10–6 M–F,
9–6 Sat, 10–4 Sun

③ Westcott to Coldharbour

☞ *The main route involves a short
stretch of the A25, as well as a bridleway
which crosses grassy fields. If this doesn't
appeal, try the alternative on page 54.*

Turn left onto the A25 and follow it for
just under half a mile, before turning off
to the right into Milton Street.

Milton Street, *like the Rookery, is only a
few yards from the teeming traffic on the A25,
but it remains a gem unknown to most of those
who dash by in their cars.*

*Immediately on the right, by the junction,
is Old Bury Hill Gardens, once the orangery
of Bury Hill House. Behind it, bordered by a
high brick wall, were the kitchen gardens.
Continuing along the lane – 'street' is far too
formal a title for it – you cross a small stream,
the Milton Brook, which then runs alongside,
so that small bridges are needed to reach the
cottages on the right.*

*Mint was grown on Milton Farm and, for
20 years around the turn of the century, there
was a peppermint distillery there. The road in
Dorking called 'Mint Gardens' is another
reminder of this short-lived industry.*

*The grounds of Bury Hill House itself are
on the left, further down the lane. The house
occupied an idyllic, sheltered position, looking
south over a large lake towards Leith Hill. It
was built in 1753 but extensively altered in*

*the 1830s. From 1803 until World War II it
was the home of the Barclays, a Quaker
family, who owned the brewery of Barclay,
Perkins & Co in Southwark.*

*The house was used by the army during
World War II and was subsequently sold for
conversion into apartments. However, during
the work a fire severely damaged the centre
part, which was subsequently demolished, and
the surviving ends were rebuilt as separate
houses. Behind the house, on top of the hill, is
an observatory, built in 1848.*

*Much of the park surrounding the house
had long been open for the public to enjoy, but
in 1930 Lt-Col R W Barclay formally gave
the 60 acres known as The Nower to the town,
to be preserved as open space.*

After the final cottage the lane passes
through a gate and becomes a narrow
bridlepath. On the left is the lake in the
grounds of Bury Hill House, held back by
a dam, which blocks your view of it. The
lake is now used for angling by the Bury
Hill Fisheries, which has created the new
Milton Lake on the other side of the path.
This occupies the site of an old osier
plantation – osiers being the type of
willow used for basket-weaving.

Cross a track which connects the old and
new lakes and then, as the path begins to
climb gently, you should be able to see over
the dam on the left. By looking back you
may be able to glimpse the surviving parts
of Bury Hill House through the trees
(4 miles).

Continue straight ahead along the path
until you come to a gate into a grassy field.
Both the bridleway and a footpath pass
through the gate and share the same route
for a few yards on the far side. The path is
quite clearly defined along the right-hand
side of the field, but the bridleway is less
obvious. It heads diagonally across the
field towards a lone oak tree. Beyond the
tree is a gate, from where a track leads to
Chadhurst Farm.

At the farm, veer slightly to the left (keep to the left of the building with timber supports) and, following the blue bridle-way arrow, take the track past the pond and uphill – it's a hefty climb – through woodland. At the top of the hill go through the gate and turn left into Logmore Lane (almost 5 miles).

☞ *The alternative route from Westcott rejoins here.*

A 500-yard climb is followed by an all-too-brief downhill run to the junction with Coldharbour Lane, where you turn right and begin climbing again. After the isolated house at Robbing Gate – note how the owners have gentrified the name – there's a more level stretch at the 6-mile mark, and a small area where cars can be parked. At the junction of Anstie Lane, follow the road to the right in the direction of 'Coldharbour & Leith Hill'. The village is about 300 yards ahead.

Coldharbour, *on the flanks of Leith Hill, claims to have the highest cricket pitch in Surrey. Other than the church, a pub, and a few cottages, there's not a great deal to the village, although the pub is sure to be welcome after the climb from Westcott.*

Just to the east of the village is Anstiebury, an Iron Age hillfort which was probably built around 200BC and used for about 150 years after that. Our understanding of these earthworks is far from complete, but it does seem that the term 'fort' is misleading. It's more likely that they were used as refuges, for use, for example, when driving cattle across country, or as trading centres.

They might have had a defensive role at times, though, and that use of Anstiebury was almost revived in the early 19th century when Napoleon threatened to invade the country. It was proposed that the people of Dorking should use the ancient site as a refuge. If it seems strange to think of a site here being so important, remember that it wasn't always

On summer Sundays and Bank Holidays, Coldharbour is served by Surrey Hills Leisure buses. A 1950s Guy Special, owned by Nostalgiabus, is seen on route 433 from Guildford.

off the beaten track. Before the main road (now the A24) was built, Coldharbour Lane was the only route into Dorking from the south, and a most unsatisfactory one at that. In 1750 the people of Horsham petitioned Parliament for the new road, as the one through Coldharbour was passable only on foot or horseback. Around 1900 the Surrey historian H E Malden wrote that he'd been told by an old man how it had been impossible for bearers to carry a coffin from Coldharbour to Dorking, so narrow was the lane at the bottom of its cutting, and so steep the sides.

The Plough, Coldharbour. Free house. 01306 711793. Open all day Sat and Sun. Excellent selection of real ales. Food

√ Coldharbour to Broadmoor Hill

Continue straight on through the village, with the mass of Leith Hill directly ahead. A short way along the lane there is an open area with a bench seat slightly up the hill on the right, from where there are magnificent views over the Weald (7 miles). Look back along the road and you can see Anstiebury above the village. At the next junction, go straight on, following the sign for 'Leith Hill'. The lane is extremely narrow, so, if you want to pause to admire the view or simply to take a breath, do pull well in.

To the right is part of Coldharbour Common, with the village war memorial – a small, simple obelisk. Pass the church and continue straight ahead at the junction beyond it. Weald View Cottages are appropriately named, but the best viewpoint is at a field-gate just beyond the cottages. Looking through, you can see Gatwick Airport in the middle distance, with the South Downs beyond, and the smoking chimneys of the local brickworks closer to. The lane bends sharply to the right and passes the Landslip car park (National Trust, but free) at Mosses Wood.

This is the best place to leave a car if you are headed for the top of Leith Hill (a ¾-mile walk), but for cyclists there's a better approach farther on. In the winter of 1995/96, the National Trust planted 100 specimen trees in Mosses Wood to mark its centenary, providing a wider range of species.

There are several bridleways and tracks leading down from the summit of Leith Hill, and they may seem more appealing than a ride along surfaced roads. We decided against them for this ride because it's easy to take a wrong turning in the woods and end up a long way from your destination.

Tanners Wood, on the right, is one of the areas which was immensely damaged by the Great Storm of 1987, when Coldharbour was cut off for days. Scrub and birch is now taking over as it regenerates.

The road bends sharply to the left, just after Cockshot Farm (8 miles). The path which branches off at the bend is the shortest route to the tower, although one of the steepest. If you wish, you can follow the signposted bridleway up to the tower, from where a bridleway to the left leads back to the road near Starveall Corner. (Alternatively, leave your bike locked up in a clearing just up the path, out of sight of the road, if you would rather walk up.)

This spot seems to be a favourite with woodpeckers – you may hear their characteristic 'drumming', but it's difficult to see them in the trees.

If you prefer not to climb to the top of the hill, look up to the right as you round the bend at Cockshot and you'll see the tower standing out above the trees. Leith Hill Place Wood is to the left of the road beyond the bend, and the National Trust has provided car parks on both sides of

Leith Hill

Leith Hill, at 965 feet, is the highest spot in south-east England. The tower was built in 1766 by Richard Hull of Leith Hill Place, to bring it up to exactly 1,000 feet and for 'the enjoyment of himself and his neighbours'. When he died six years later, he was buried beneath its floor. The tower was then virtually abandoned and, after its doors, windows and other fittings had been stolen, it was filled in with cement. What does that say about Hull's neighbours? The tower was heightened in 1788 and then restored in 1864, when the battlements and turreted staircase were added.

Even without the extra height provided by the tower, John Aubrey, the 17th century antiquary, reckoned that the circumference of the horizon visible from the top of the hill could not be less than 200 miles. In his diaries, John Evelyn claimed that 'from it may be discerned twelve or thirteen counties on a serene day'. They must both have been very fortunate in their choice of days for visiting, though today's pollution is a major cause of the haze which tends to restrict the view.

In 1847, Leith Hill Place was bought by Josiah Wedgwood, a descendant of the man who founded the famous pottery firm. He was married to the sister of Charles Darwin, who is said to have conducted experiments in the earth-moving capabilities of worms hereabouts. Wedgwood's daughter married the

Rev A Vaughan Williams, and the house passed into the ownership of that family. In 1944 they donated the house and the surrounding lands to the National Trust.

Ralph Vaughan Williams, the composer, and his sister Margaret were deeply involved in the annual Leith Hill Music Festival, which was founded in 1904 and is still going strong. (Despite its name, the festival is based in Dorking.)

Leith Hill tower is open from April to September on Wednesdays 12–5, and on Saturdays, Sundays and Bank Holidays 11–5. Last admission is at 4.30. It is also open at weekends between October and March 11–3.30, with last admission at 3.00. Entry costs 50p. The tower has an information room and a telescope.

the road at Windy Gap. At the next junction, take the right fork (the marked road). The signpost here has been turned (or blown) around, but it should point to 'Abinger Common & Wotton'. Another junction follows within 100 yards or so. Turn right, up an 11 per cent hill. To the left, immediately after the junction, is an entrance into the National Trust's Rhododendron Wood. (Entrance is free, and a visit in May or June is highly recommended.)

☞ *To link with Ride A, instead of heading uphill, turn left onto the narrow Tanhurst Lane, which heads downhill to Forest Green.*

Further signs of the 1987 storm, in the form of shattered trees, can be seen as you climb the hill towards Starveall Corner and its car park (almost 9 miles). Pass the entrance to High Ashes Farm, then, at the next junction, turn right in the direction of 'Broadmoor'.

☞ *To join Ride B, continue straight ahead at this junction.*

An undulating half-mile of lane leads to Leylands Farm, after which a downhill stretch takes you past Wotton Barn and Leylands (10 miles), once the home of Arthur Brooke, whose father founded the Brooke Bond tea empire. Look out on the left, just beyond the house, for a truly magnificent beech tree. A level ride past Severells Copse, now in the ownership of the National Trust, brings you back to Broadmoor Hill car park (10½ miles).

Alternative section of route

③ Westcott to Coldharbour

☞ *This alternative route avoids both the ride along the A25 and the bridleway which crosses farm fields.*

Turn right from the green onto the A25 for the short distance to the Cricketers pub by Westcott Heath. Turn left here, following the sign to Logmore Lane. Keep to the main, marked road, climbing steeply past the church and ignoring Heath Rise on the left. At the junction beyond the church, by Wescott Hill House, veer left into Logmore Lane, where the slope levels out.

Keep an eye out for Logmore Place – look through the gateway in the hedge opposite for a superb view over the countryside towards Dorking. On the far hillside, about a mile off, can be seen Bury Hill House and its observatory. From a little further along the lane, opposite the turning to Logmore Green, you can see the tall blocks of flats which are the landmark of North Holmwood, to the south of Dorking.

Continue along the lane past Westlees Farm, from where it climbs for a short distance. (This stretch is rather badly potholed.) It soon enters an area of woodland, through which the road twists and climbs, quite steeply in parts. The main route is rejoined at the entrance to Chadhurst Farm.

Ride D:
'On the road to Ewood'

Capel • Rusper • Russ Hill • Charlwood • Stan Hill • Monks Lake • Cudworth
• Parkgate • Ewood • Henfold • Newdigate • Capel

Distance: 25 miles
Landranger Maps: 187
Pathfinder Maps: 1226, 1227, 1246, 1247

The part of Surrey between the A23 and A24 is countryside of surprising contrasts. On one hand, Gatwick Airport and the expanding towns of Crawley and Horley are bringing about greatly increased traffic on country roads, as well as a spread of suburbanisation which is being resisted only with some difficulty. On the other, you can still find tiny hamlets which were among the earliest settlements in the Weald forests and, even today, some of them can be reached only by rough tracks.

Ewood is one of these. Once the most important settlement in the area (so much so that the name of today's thriving village of Newdigate means 'on the road to Ewood'), it is now hidden away, totally off the beaten track.

Another contrast is the way in which modern housing developments exist alongside a rich assortment of buildings from bygone ages. That so many old buildings have survived is the result of the changing economic fortunes of the area. When new methods of smelting using coal, instead of charcoal, were invented, the Surrey iron-making industry collapsed, and two hundred years of prosperity were followed by hard times in the 18th and 19th centuries.

Improved agricultural methods – the salvation of many rural communities – were of little practical value on the heavy clay soil and brought no relief. As a result, the houses built during the good times remained in much their original condition, because there was little money to improve or replace them. Most have lasted to this day for our enjoyment.

Special Note

Some of the off-road sections of this ride are very rough and can be hard going, no matter what the weather. If you don't have a mountain bike (and a well-padded saddle) there are some stretches you may want to walk. Unfortunately, these are the very tracks which take you to the out-of-the-way spots which are central to this ride, so there is little point in offering alternative routes. Allow a full day so that you can take it easy if you want to.

Starting Points

Start at Capel, off the A24 Dorking–Horsham road. There are no official car parks but parking on the road by the small

Ride D
'On the road to Ewood'

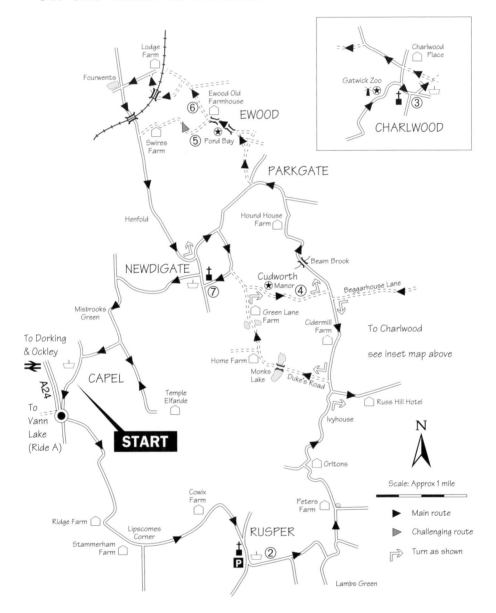

green at the south end of the village (grid ref TQ 173402) seems unlikely to cause problems. There is also a small car park next to the church in Rusper, where the ride strays over the border into West Sussex.

⇌ The nearest station is at Ockley, on the Dorking–Horsham line, which is operated by Connex South Central (see Ride C). Turn left out of the station approach onto the B2126 and follow it to the junction with the A24. Cross the A24 to reach the Capel turning. Turn right at The Street in Capel to join the route.

The Route in Brief

① Head south along The Street to A24, then TL off roundabout, SP Rusper. Continue SO for 4 miles. At TJ at end of lane TR for Rusper.

② FL at The Star pub then TL at next junc. Pass turning to Lambs Green then TL at next junc, SP The Mount & Newdigate. Ignore next on R, then TR at TJ, SP Charlwood. At next turning TR, SP Russ Hill & Charlwood. Pass Hotel and Zoo, then TR at TJ.

③ TL into Chapel Road then, at junc with Swan Lane, continue SO onto BY. At junc of paths follow track to L. At road SO into Stan Hill, then at top of hill TL into Beggarhouse Lane, SP Greenings. At Eastlands cottage continue SO onto unmade BY. At far end TL onto road for 1 mile then TR at East Lodge of Newdigate Place onto Dukes Road – unmade track (BW).

Cross bridge between two lakes and follow old carriage drive to Home Farm. Pass farm buildings and go straight ahead past oak tree. Do not join farm drive. Pass through tubular gate (note BW sign) and along edge of field. Go through second gate and aim slightly left of ahead across next field.

Follow track out of field and through Green Lane Farm.

At next junc TR into Cudworth Estate (also BW). Follow lane for about 1 mile past Cudworth Manor to road.

√ TL onto road for about 2 miles, passing junc with Blanks Lane, to Parkgate. TR into Broad Lane then L immediately into Mill Lane. Continue onto unmade track for about 300 yds to start of private road then TL onto clay path through woods, signed as BW. After another 300 yds FL along bottom of garden and across gravel drive (still BW). At road TL.

⑤ *via Swires Farm*
TL beside fence immediately before barn of Ewood Old Farmhouse and follow path across field, keeping to L of hedge. At far end go through tubular gate and cross small bridge into long, narrow field. TR, keep R of clump of trees then aim for L side of field. Follow tracks to far end of field then TL out through gate. Follow farm track through farmyard from where concrete track leads onto road from Fourwents. TL and follow directions in ≈ .

≈ *via Fourwents*
Continue SO past Ewood Old Farmhouse then FR at edge of woods. At end of woods continue SO when another track merges from R. TL onto lengthy BW diversion along concrete track, passing under railway to reach Lodge Farm, then TL onto road. At Fourwents Pond XR TL, SP Newdigate. Route via Swires Farm (see ⑤) joins from L just after railway bridge.

At TJ TL, SP Leigh & Charlwood, then TR into New Barn Lane. At next junc follow road round to R.

Δ At church TR then take next on L, SP Capel & Beare Green. TL at following TJ for Capel.

The Ride

① Capel to Rusper

Capel was originally known as Ewekene, a name which still survives in that of a farm just to the north of the village. It got its present name thanks to the chapel (in Latin 'capella') which was built there in the 12th century. It didn't last long though; it was replaced by the present church about 100 years later, and this, in turn, was mostly rebuilt in 1865.

The village street was, not so long ago, the main A24 road, but fortunately it has now been bypassed and you can enjoy a walk round in reasonable peace and quiet. There's not much outstanding to see but a lot that's interesting. Most local guidebooks mention the almshouses built in memory of Charles Webb of Clapham Common but none explain his connection with the village. The Old Post Office and the Old Stores are also worth a glance; their fascination lies in the odd way they're joined together. There are several other picturesque cottages, some tucked well back from the road.

The Crown Inn, The Street. Free house. 01306 711130. Open all day. Food G
Patels, The Street. Off licence
Holmcroft Nursery & General Store, The Street.

To link with Ride A take the bridleway which starts at the NW corner of the Clark's Green roundabout by the entrance to Grenehurst Park. Follow it over the railway to Weare Street.

From the village head south along The Street, up the rise to the roundabout on the A24 at Clark's Green, then take the turning for Rusper and pass the green after which the spot is named. Clark's Farm, just beyond, is now derelict. In the distance, on the right, is a large brickworks. After the entrance to Pleystowe Farm (1 mile) there is a gentle downhill run past a clay pit from which the raw

material for the brickworks is obtained. Thankfully, it's well screened by trees.

The descent becomes steeper beyond the entrance to Taylors, a farmhouse dating back to the 15th century, ending at a bridge over a small stream. A short climb on the other side brings you to the entrance to Ridge Farm (2 miles), after which the road bends to the left and dips to cross another stream, with a long slope up on the far side. Stammerham Farm, still a working farm but with some of its buildings now converted into a business centre, is about half way up the hill. The farm is in West Sussex and for the next mile, the road is the county boundary.

The change of county is obvious at the next junction, Lipscomes Corner. West Sussex has abandoned the use of ugly modern signposts on quieter roads and has restored many of the old ones, an idea which other councils should surely be encouraged to follow. Note the erratic distances on this example, though. Capel and Rusper are nearly 4 miles apart, but each is shown as being 1 mile distant!

Go straight on at the junction, unless you want to divert to the Royal Oak pub, which is about half a mile off to the right.

The long climb eases after the junction. There are woods on the left, but to the right are splendid views across a shallow valley to a ridge of hills. An undulating stretch of road follows, past the cottages at Cowix Farm, which are about 3¼ miles from the start.

The road bends to the right and heads firmly into West Sussex at a spot called Waffles Corner, and soon afterwards passes a lovely house called Highams, with its roof made from slabs of Horsham stone. At the next junction turn right for Rusper. The road passes the Ghyll Manor Country Club, Hotel & Restaurant, and then enters the village itself (4 miles).

Rusper

Rusper: *The Plough Inn dates from the 15th century and was once part of a hospice run by nuns from the neighbouring Benedictine Nunnery, the original building of which was demolished in 1781. When additions to the present 19th century building were made some years ago, several graves were unearthed, being those of a Prioress and several sisters. The church of St Mary Magdalene has a medieval tower; the rest was rebuilt in 1855, but to the original design.*

Look out for the house called Averys, on the Horsham Road opposite the Star Inn. It was built around 1550 and, until the early 19th century, was the home of the village blacksmith. John Avery improved the house and divided it up, leasing it to local traders. When the local mill burned down, the miller moved into the barn at the back of the building, installing steam-driven equipment.

Plough, High Street. 01293 871215. Food

The Star, High Street. 01293 871264. Food. G

Rusper Village Stores and Post Office, 6.30–5.30 (Sat 7–1, Sun 9–1)

② Rusper to Charlwood

Follow the road through Rusper, taking the left fork (the major road) at The Star pub. At the following junction turn left into a fairly narrow lane. (The turning is not signposted but is at a sharp right bend in the road, by a house called Rosecroft.) The lane is often used as short-cut to Crawley, so take care.

After a sharp bend to the right, you'll come to a junction with the lane to Lambs Green (just over 5 miles); continue on the main road in the direction of Ifield. Just after a left-hand bend take the next turning on the left, signposted to 'The Mount & Newdigate'.

This is a single-track lane which climbs steadily uphill for nearly half a mile until it comes to another junction. With its traditional signpost on a grassy island in the middle, a pond nearby, and a couple of farms, it's an attractive spot, spoiled only by being directly under the Gatwick flight-path. The signpost is slightly misleading as you can reach Charlwood in either of two directions, so continue straight ahead. A sign outside Peters Farm, a timber-framed house on the left, says that it was built in 1570. Notice how the roof is made partly of Horsham stone and partly of tile.

Beyond the entrance to Gotwick Farm (almost 6 miles) the road runs past a gill, which, considering it was formed by only a small stream, is quite deep. An uphill climb leads to a junction where the ride's diversion into West Sussex comes to an end. On the left is a barn constructed half in brick and half in timber, and on the right an attractive house called Orltons. Turn right, in the direction signposted 'Charlwood', and look at the side of the house as you pass. A much older house is built into the side of it.

The road runs along a high ridge here and, where the hedges allow, there are good views towards the North Downs. Since the ride is now back in Surrey there are none of the attractive old signposts to be seen, except in the garden of a cottage on the right. In one direction it points to 'Ivyhouse Cottages' and in the other to 'The Rest of the World'!

The 7-mile point is about halfway between the entrance of Oaklands Park and the turning to Russ Hill and Charlwood. Turn right and head downhill into a slight dip, over a stream, and back up the other side. The wood on the left, called Glover's Wood, is partly owned by the Woodland Trust, a charitable organisation which seeks to acquire, preserve and manage woods and forest land throughout the country for the public to use and enjoy. The Trust welcomes volunteer help in maintaining the woods and their paths and details of forthcoming working parties will be found by the entrance gate.

The need to save the countryside in this area is well illustrated by the mess that is the Russ Hill Hotel. The view of the back of the hotel is definitely uninspiring, and although the front is rather better, it is dominated by car parks.

Beyond the hotel is the entrance to Russ Hill Farm (just under 8 miles). Pause at the entrance (by the stile where the Sussex Border Path goes off) to look down from this vantage point onto Gatwick Airport below.

Follow the road downhill and you'll soon see a white-painted windmill on the left. It once stood at Lowfield Heath, south of the airport, beside the A23, but was brought here to a site adjacent to Gatwick Zoo for preservation and restoration. It's a post mill dating from the middle of the 18th century. The inside is open on summer Sunday afternoons; admission is free.

Gatwick Zoo: *The zoo houses a collection of exotic species, including otters, penguins, flamingoes and monkeys, and a wide variety of birds, plants, and butterflies in its 10-acre country site. It is open daily from 10.30 (Mar–Oct to 6, Nov–Feb to 4 with reduced facilities).* ☎ *01293 862312 for more information.*

Beyond the zoo, there are some delightful houses on the final stretch of road as it runs into Charlwood. Robbins Farm is interesting for the fact that it has a Horsham stone roof at the front but tile at the sides. Bristow Cottage, on the left, is a delightful but tiny cottage, with what you feel must be an overbearing weight of its stone roof. Laurel Cottage would also be delightful but for the unsympathetic flat-roofed extension at the back.

Charlwood

Charlwood is too close to Gatwick Airport for comfort, and it will be a lot less pleasant if the airport gets the go-ahead for its second runway. One scheme put forward would see the village sandwiched between the two runways! But, in the face of this possible devastation, it works hard at maintaining its rural atmosphere, and it won a Best Kept Village award to prove it.

St Nicholas's Church, which dates from Norman times, is famous for its wall paintings, which were discovered in 1858 when the whitewash covering them was removed. One depicts the story of St Margaret, another an incident from the life of St Nicholas, and the third a morality tale. After being uncovered they began to fade, a process hastened by a treatment which was meant to preserve them. Happily they were restored in the 1960s. The porch has an attractive sundial added in 1791, but you'll notice how the 18th century craftsman who carved the motto wasn't too well up on his Latin, so we have Tempest Fugit. The storm flies, not the time!

The path through the graveyard is one of the famous local 'causies', paths or causeways made of stone flags to keep walkers out of the clay. They can be found in several places in the village.

One of the oddest sights in Charlwood is the Providence Chapel. The wooden building looks as if it's from the set of a wild west movie. Its date, 1816, looks right for the period too. In fact, it was a Napoleonic–era barracks hut from Horsham. With the victory at Waterloo in 1815, the barracks were no longer needed and this hut was moved to Charlwood for a more peaceful use.

At the end of the road, opposite the Parish Hall (9 miles), turn right into the centre of Charlwood village. Go past the turning on the right marked 'No Entry' and then take the next right turn. This loop off the main street serves one of the village pubs, the Half Moon, and the church.

In his *Highways and Byways in Surrey*, Eric Parker described how two pollarded elms were once trained into an arch across the entrance to this road. (Is this why the adjacent house is called Temple Bar?) Sadly, one of the trees was hit by a lorry in the 1930s, and the other also had to be removed.

▦ *The Half Moon, The Street. Friary Meux. 01293 862902. Open 11–11. Food*
▦ *The Rising Sun, The Street. Charringtons. 01293 862338. Open all day (Sun 12.30–10) Food (all day menu until 8.30) G*
⌂ *Charles, The Street. Newsagent, off-licence and food store.*

From The Street divert briefly into Rosemary Lane (on the left beside the Rising Sun pub) where you'll find the 18th century village cage, in which local offenders were once incarcerated. It has two small barred but unglazed windows and apparently also has bars in the roof. Were they added after the occupants of a similar building in Lingfield were rescued through its roof or did the authorities in Charlwood simply have greater foresight?

③ Charlwood to Cudworth

After the diversion into Rosemary Lane continue along The Street for about 100 yards, then turn left into Chapel Road. At the far end, at the junction with Swan Lane, continue straight ahead onto the public byway. Look ahead and slightly to the right and you can see the town of Horley in the distance. The fascinating Providence Chapel is a little further along on the left.

☞ *The first part of the track is bes described as worn, but after the chapel i becomes rough. If you'd rather not risk your bike, turn around and retrace your steps through the village. At the Parish Hall, rather than turning off into Rectory Lane, continue straight ahead to the junction with Stan Hill, where the other end of the track emerges.*

At the junction with some paths, follow the track around to the left. The next stretch is known as Pudding Lane. Ahead, just to the right, you can see the extensive modern farm buildings which occupy most of the site of Charlwood Place, home of the Saunders or Sanders family who moved there from Sanderstead in the early 14th century.

Continue your bumpy way along the track past Spottles Farm to its junction with the road (10 miles). Cross into Stan Hill, following the sign for Newdigate. The road's name is appropriate. Meaning 'Stone Hill', it refers to a ridge of limestone sticking up out of the clay. At the top turn left into Beggarhouse Lane, which is signposted 'Greenings'.

The first part of the lane is tarred, but at the lovely cottage called 'Eastlands' continue straight ahead onto the unmade byway. Here we are faced with an intriguing situation. In legal terms, a byway is a right of way which is open to all types of traffic. However, here the local authority has banned not only cars and motorbikes but even horse-drawn carts!

The byway is a dirt track, but in good condition, although it might be dusty in dry conditions. It has deep ditches on either side which should help to keep it well drained in wet weather. It is lined with trees and overgrown hedges at first, but soon it emerges into the open near Greenings Farm (just over 11 miles). There are marvellous views towards the North

Downs. On the left of the Mole gap, the spire of the church at Ranmore can be seen on top of the Downs, while on the right is the steep slope of Box Hill and further along are the white scars of the chalk quarries around Brockham and Betchworth.

Beyond the open fields the track passes through a wooded stretch before coming out onto the road (Partridge Lane).

☞ *From here the ride follows a 3½-mile loop through Cudworth. Most of it is along rough farm tracks but there is one stretch across a farm field which could be extremely challenging after wet weather. It's a worthwhile and interesting ride, and highly recommended, but if you'd rather avoid it, turn right and rejoin the main route about 200 yards along the road at the end of Burnt Oak Lane (see stage √).*

No horse-drawn carts!

Turn left onto Partridge Lane for about a mile. There is a gentle climb uphill at first, passing Rolls Farm and other houses. At the top of the hill the lane bends slightly and passes Cidermill Farm. This stretch of lane is quite deserted and peaceful and, after the dirt track of Beggarhouse Lane, it's a pleasure to bowl along on a tarred surface. Enjoy it while it lasts!

When you come to the East Lodge of Newdigate Place, turn right into the unmade track called Dukes Road. (The bridleway sign has been broken but it is assuredly a right of way.) Newdigate Place is on the right, its entrance about 200 yards from the lodge. The original Victorian mansion, built in 1897, was used by the Army during the Second World War, and was left so derelict and damaged that it had to be demolished. Its replacement is no more than a bungalow.

The track heads down a gentle slope through mixed woodland and fields. Its surface is in fair condition: a little rough in places, but, in the main, the riding is easy. The land through which the track passes was once a deer park. The Duke after whom the track is named was the Duke of Norfolk, who owned the Manor of Newdigate in the early 19th century.

About half a mile from the lodge the track approaches a house in the trees on the left – Monks Lake Farm (13 miles). Pass the farm entrance and the lake itself comes into view on the left. There is another to the right, with a brick-built spillway linking the two.

The track crosses the spillway by a bridge, the parapets of which are rather decayed. The bridge itself may be in no better state, since two massive sections of tree trunk have been placed to stop vehicles crossing it. Just before the bridge the main track curves to the right into a car parking area for an angling club. Pause for a moment to

Monks Lake

enjoy the scene, the existence of which few people are aware.

When you're ready, continue straight ahead, crossing the bridge and passing around the end of the gate which blocks the track just beyond. The gate leads onto what was once the main driveway to Newdigate Place. It's lined with iron fencing and neat hedges and passes through an avenue of Scots Pines. It must have looked quite grand in its time but today seems sadly neglected.

The drive leads to Home Farm, which was the original Newdigate Place. Pass the farm buildings and continue straight ahead past the oak tree on the right. Do not join the farm drive – instead, go through the tubular steel gate in front of you; it has a sign saying 'Please shut gate' and there is a bridleway marker on a fence post on the right.

Go along the edge of the field past some derelict outbuildings and through a second tubular gate into another field. Head slightly left of ahead across this field. If you look carefully you'll see a stile in the hedge at the far end; aim for a point just to its left.

The field is rough pasture grazed by cows, and is extremely bumpy. You will find it much less uncomfortable if you push your bike, and at the same time you'll avoid any risk of upsetting calves in the field. As you near the end of the field, you'll see a clearly-marked track leading to the gate.

Beyond the gate, the track has a reasonable surface. It passes through an area where, at the time of writing, some new ponds were being landscaped. Continue along the track to a gate into the farmyard of Green Lane Farm. Go straight through the farmyard and out by the gates

Cudworth

Cudworth is probably one of the oldest settlements in the area covered by this ride, but you'll be hard-pressed to find mention of it in most Surrey guide books. Its name is Anglo-Saxon in origin, meaning 'Cudda's Ford', and appeared in documents dated 1229 as Cudiford.

In 1902 the estate was purchased by the Small Holders Association and divided up into plots for sale to people who wanted to build a house and farm a few acres, an idea which became popular with early Socialists in particular. The 1997 BBC television series *Plotlands* told the story of a similar, though fictional, estate. Cudworth Park was the site of one of the first holiday camps in the country. Now a mobile home park, it originally provided tents for its guests.

Cudworth Manor is set on a moated site and is reached by a covered bridge which has a dovecot set into its roof. The earliest surviving part of the building – the central portion – dates to around 1500 but there have been many alterations and additions over the years. Ironically, on the side nearest the moat, the timber-framing of the oldest part of the building has been replaced by brick, while the part which is timber-framed was built between the First and Second World Wars.

The manor is quite a superb sight and one of the few places in Surrey where it is possible for the public to get close enough to a moated house to appreciate it.

at the far end, past the old red (non-operational) telephone box. Pass the modern bungalows and leave the farm, crossing a small bridge (14 miles). Continue along the farm drive for 200 yards or so to a junction, then turn right into the Cudworth Estate, keeping an eye out for the speed humps.

Follow the private lane through the estate. There are a few houses grouped around the start of the lane, but then there is an open downhill stretch leading to Cudworth Manor, with the moated house on the left and the Beam Brook on the right.

Continue straight ahead, going to the left of the large wooden barn, past the entrance to Cudworth Manor Farm, and by the pond. From there follow the lane on past Ash Cottage. The entrance to Cudworth Park is on the left after a couple of hundred yards.

Some of the last houses along the lane – which, east of the Manor, is known as Burnt Oak Lane – are hidden away behind high fences and gates (15 miles).

√ Cudworth to Ewood

Turn left at the end of Burnt Oak Lane into Partridge Lane and enjoy the run downhill to the small bridge over the Beam Brook. This area has been prone to flooding over the years, which must suit the aquatic nurseries but not the residents of Old Beam Brook.

From there the road climbs up a slight rise to Sturtwood Farm, where the road bends sharply to the left. Further along, on the right, is The Red House (16 miles), now used as office premises. The original late Victorian building of this name was largely demolished and rebuilt after the war, when, like Newdigate Place, it was badly damaged during use by the Army. Next door is The Clock House, formerly the

stable block. The clock was once on the wall facing the road, but has now been removed. It was placed there in the 1970s when the owner tired of being asked the time by the eccentric occupant of Hound House Farm opposite, who possessed no clocks or watches. Much of Hound House Farm itself was sadly destroyed in a fire in 1981, but the end nearest the road survived and has been incorporated in a new house on the site.

There is another gentle downhill stretch past Coombers Farm, which leads to the junction with Blanks Lane. On the right just before this junction there used to stand a tiny cottage which consisted of one room downstairs with a second room in the attic space above, reached by a ladder. Although this one probably dated from about 1600, it was a remarkable survival, in virtually its original condition, of a typical villager's cottage of the 14th or 15th century. Sadly, it was demolished in 1965. Had it lasted a few more years it would undoubtedly have been preserved for posterity. The house called Little Cherryhurst was built on its site and took its name.

At the junction continue straight ahead in the direction signposted 'Newdigate'. Shortly after the junction, look out on the right for Partridge Cottage, once an ale house known as Sots Hole. The comedian Frankie Howerd lived there for a while after the Second World War and gave it its present name. Just across the road is Pear Tree Cottage, presumably named by someone with a subtle sense of humour.

After a short climb, the road comes to Parkgate and the junction with Broad Lane. The route turns right here, but as opportunities for refreshment are few and far between on the ride, you may wish to carry straight on for a short distance to the Surrey Oaks pub. Having quenched your thirst, return to the junction.

The Surrey Oaks, Parkgate Road. Friary Meux. 01306 631200. Food G

Turn into Broad Lane, then left into Mill Lane almost immediately. The first part of the road has recently been made up with pavements, following the building of an estate of executive homes (Beckett Wood) on the site of the Schermuly Pistol Rocket Apparatus factory. This made flares, rockets and line-throwing apparatus, but it closed in 1981 following a takeover by Pains (of fireworks fame), who moved the production to Salisbury.

Beyond the new development Mill Lane becomes an unmade track (just under 17 miles). Follow this for about 300 yards until you come to a junction. The road ahead is signed as private, and a bridleway sign directs you to the left onto a clay path through the woods. The path seems to be well-used by horse riders and could cause a few difficulties in very wet weather.

After another 300 yards or so, take the left fork when the track divides just before a wooden bungalow. The path runs along the bottom of the garden of the bungalow and then, to reach the road beyond, it crosses the gravel drive between the bungalow and some sheds. Don't be put off by this apparent diversion onto private property. As you'll see by the sign when you reach the road, this is most definitely a public right of way.

Turn left when you get to the road. It's reasonably well-surfaced, although there are numerous potholes which have been filled with a variety of rubble and quantities of broken tiles, so take care.

The road passes a couple of cottages and dips to cross a bridge over a stream. There is a blue bridleway arrow on a post just after the bridge. On the left is Mill Cottage at Ewood. Look at the bottom of the garden to the left of the cottage and you'll see the dam (or 'pond bay' as it's usually

termed), with steps cut into it. The dam continues behind and to the right of the cottage. From Mill Cottage the lane crosses a second bridge and heads towards Ewood Old Farmhouse.

☞ At this point you must choose your onward route. The challenging way is to follow a bridleway across the fields and then via Ewood Lane through Swires Farm (see stage ⑤). It's rough and bumpy and could be quite difficult after heavy rain. The sensible way is to continue along the farm drive (see stage ≈).

⑤ Ewood to Newdigate
via Swires farm

As you approach Ewood Old Farmhouse, turn left beside the fence immediately before the barn. Another blue bridleway arrow marks the way. It leads onto a fairly well-defined path running across a field. Away to the left you can see the new houses on the site of the old factories; between you and them is the site of the mill pond. At the time of writing, a contractors' access track crossed the bridleway about halfway over the field. Cross this track and continue along the path (keep to the left of the hedge) until you come to a tubular metal gate at the far end of the field.

Go through the gate and cross a small bridge into a long but narrow field. Turn right, keeping to the right of the small clump of trees and the adjacent fenced-in pond (18 miles). Then aim towards the left-hand side of the field. Beside the hedge you'll find some tractor tracks, which are easier to ride on than the rough pasture.

At the far end of the field follow the track around to the left and out of the field through a gate. From there, the track takes you to the farmyard at Swires Farm. Go straight ahead across the farmyard and past the modern barn with grey metal

Ewood
Remnants of Surrey's industrial past

Looking at it now, it's hard to believe that this tiny out-of-the-way hamlet was once one of the most important industrial centres of Surrey – indeed, of the whole country. It was the iron industry which brought about its prosperity. Documents dated 1553 record that an iron mill, believed to be the first in Surrey, was already well-established at Ewood. All the materials needed for its production were here in plenty: ironstone, found in the local soils; wood for making charcoal, which burns with a fierce heat; and ample surface water to provide the power.

Ewood was one of the few places in the country specifically exempted from Acts of 1558 and 1581 which limited the felling of trees. Iron-making required vast quantities of timber and most ironmasters simply cut down trees which were needed for many other purposes, including the building of ships and houses. The works at Ewood, however, seem to have had an efficiently-managed system of coppiced woodland which produced a renewable crop of timber.

Even so, the costs of firewood and charcoal in the area nearly doubled by 1562. Incidentally, the name of a local farm, Collaroy, may derive from the word *collier*, which originally meant charcoal-burner.

Iron was smelted by putting the ironstone into a furnace fired by charcoal. Once the metal was melted it was drawn off in long lumps called pigs or sows. These were then pounded by a massive hammer, not only to beat them into a usable shape but also to help remove impurities. Ironworks consisted of two parts – the furnace and the hammer (also known as the forge). They were often, but not invariably situated together. Both used water power, the furnace to drive the bellows, and the forge to power the hammer. The power came from a waterwheel fed by a large pond, which was created by building a dam across a stream in a shallow valley.

The main pond at Ewood was between 80 and 100 acres in size, and there were other smaller ones which may have been intended to provide additional water capacity. The substantial dam of the main pond – it was over 200 yards long – can still be seen immediately behind the Mill Cottage. The 17th century antiquarian John Aubrey recorded that the pond could easily be seen from the top of Holmbury Hill.

After iron-making ceased here in around 1610 the pond was used to power a water mill and was also stocked with fish. However, it appears that it was drained, bit by bit, during the late 18th and early 19th centuries and today, apart from the dam and an unusually large field, nothing of it remains.

doors. From there a concrete track passes the farmhouse and leads to the road, where you join the route via Fourwents. Turn left and follow the directions given in stage ≈ below.

≈ **Ewood to Newdigate** *via Fourwents*

Follow the track between Ewood Old Farmhouse and the adjacent barn. The track, which is in a rather rough state, climbs a fairly steep slope past Parkwood Cottage. When it divides at the edge of some woods just after the cottage, take the right-hand fork – you can see the track heading straight into the distance. On the right along the next stretch are woods (about 18 miles), and if you are fortunate and quiet, you might see a deer.

At the end of the woods another track joins from the right. From here, the way ahead seems to be straight up the hill towards a white-painted house by the railway. However, the level crossing has been closed and the right of way diverted to the left along a new concrete road, which is signed as a bridleway.

Follow this road as it curves around and passes under the railway by a bridge. On the other side of the bridge it heads up a slight slope towards Lodge Farm, where it meets the public road. Turn left, passing Hawesrew Farm (19 miles).

Continue along the road until you come to the crossroads at the end opposite Fourwents Pond. Turn left here, in the direction signposted 'Newdigate'.

A gentle uphill climb takes you past Wymbleton Farm. Watch out for Posterns Court, on the left at the top of the slope, the front of which is dominated by a very large, decorative window. After the

Ewood Old Farmhouse

railway bridge the road passes the entrance to Swires Farm, where the alternative route (see stage ⑤) rejoins.

☞ *Distances given from this point are those via Fourwents. The route through Swires Farm is almost a mile shorter, although the rougher conditions amply make up for this!*

There is a pleasant downhill stretch past Stockrydons (20 miles) as far as the bridge by the entrance to Henfold Lakes fishery. The climb up from the bridge starts easily enough but then it steepens to 17 per cent (greater than 1 in 6) for a short distance. This is Henfold Hill, formed of iron-bearing gravels.

At the top of the climb is the hamlet of Henfold – Henfold House is followed by Henfold Farm, and then Henfold Cottages (21 miles), all once part of the Henfold Estate, which was owned during the later part of the 19th century by the Farnell-Watson family. They had made their wealth through the Isleworth Brewery and bought up a considerable amount of land in and around Newdigate.

Gosscroft Cottage, on the left a short distance further on, is a fascinating building. The front elevation is tiled and looks relatively modern, but the side, which shows the timber-framing, reveals it to be very much older – probably dating back as far as the early 1400s. It was once an inn called 'The Pussy Cat'.

The road crosses a stream and then climbs a slope past the recreation ground to the main road. The farmhouse by the junction is called Brooklag Farm, which is probably an Anglo-Saxon name meaning 'settlement by a stream'. The centre of Newdigate is only a couple of hundred yards away on the right, but a better idea is to turn left (in the direction of Leigh and Charlwood) and circle round the village to enjoy it better.

Gaterounds Farm, on the left, is certainly not to be missed. Indeed, it's worth a second and even a third look. Immediately beside the house, with a wall along one edge, is a delightful pond.

Just beyond Gaterounds, turn right into a road which is known both as New Barn Lane and, rather more quaintly, Hogspudding Lane. Spaciously-sited houses, most of which are modern, line the right-hand side of the lane, but along the opposite side is the site of the Newdigate Brickworks and its associated claypits. One of these is now flooded and is used for fishing (22 miles).

In 1995 plans were submitted to build a new brickworks here but, not surprisingly, there was considerable local protest. The outcome was awaited at the time of writing.

At the next junction, by Oakfield House (a rather pleasant Edwardian building), follow the road round to the right. Simons, on the left, used to be called Horsielands – the name has now been assumed by the adjacent farmhouse, built in 1922. Dean House Farm, on the right just beyond a small pond, has a prominently-advertised farm shop. Opposite is George Horley Place, built on the site of the old village school. Immediately before the church is the Old Rectory, now a nursing home.

▦ *The Six Bells. Free house. 01306 631276. Food*
☕ *Lisa's Bakery and Coffee Shop. Open to 7pm Mon–Fri (6pm Sat, 5pm Sun)*
🛒 *Bettesworths. Store and post office. Open to 6.30pm (6pm Wed, 1.30pm Sat/Sun)*

Opposite the end of Church Lane is a delightful grouping of buildings centred on the Six Bells pub. To the left are White Cottage and Old Cottage; the centre section of this pair of houses was originally one house. Extensions were built on each end in the 17th century and

Newdigate

Newdigate began as little more than a scattering of farms and houses along the road to Ewood. Even today, the long, narrow shape of the parish reflects its origins. The Domesday Book says nothing about Newdigate, which was then part of the ill-defined outlying lands of the Manors of Reigate and Dorking. After the Conquest these manors were granted to William de Warenne when he was made Earl of Surrey.

De Warenne may have established its first church – a wayside chapel. When the present building was begun is not clear. A document of around 1163, in the British Museum, talks of the chapel (capella) of Newdigate, but by the end of that century reference was being made to both a church and a chapel. The chancel was extended in around 1200 and the south aisle was added 50 years later. The timber tower was built in the early 15th century. Another change took place late in the 19th century when the north aisle was added. Inside the church is the old parish chest, carved out of a single piece of wood, and possibly dating from about the time the tower was added.

The village has a couple of shops and a pub, the Six Bells. There is an active Newdigate Society which produced a fascinating guide to the parish, and in 1993 a more extensive book *Newdigate – Its History and Houses* was written and published by two local residents. It is packed with valuable information for those who want to know more about the area and its buildings. One old building you'll not see, however, is the Old Bakehouse. It was dismantled in 1988 and taken to the Weald and Downland Open Air Museum at Singleton, near Chichester.

it was divided up. At one time it was known as Six Bells Cottages and provided homes for several families. On the other side of the pub is Yew Tree Cottage.

Δ Newdigate to Ewood

Turn right at the Six Bells (signposted 'Beare Green') and go along the Street for about 200 yards, before turning left into Trig Street, which is signposted 'Capel and Beare Green'. On the right are the Village Hall and the tiny cottage called Brocus, which is also the name given to the fields behind them; they were bought by the village as a war memorial and are used as a sports and recreation ground.

Kingsland Farm, on the left, has a lovely small pond in its front garden (almost 23 miles). Kingsland Cottage and Bay Cottage (another case of one house being extended and then divided in two) also used to have a pond in the garden. As the house had no well, the pond was used as the water supply!

The entrance to Greens Farm is on the left, a short distance beyond Kingsland, but the farmhouse is tucked away nearly half a mile from the road. This is a pity, because it is thought to be one of the earliest surviving houses in Surrey, let alone Newdigate. Several features suggest it was built before 1300.

On the other side of the road, an overgrown earth bank hides more quarry workings, which continue all the way to the next T-junction. Turn left here, in the direction of Capel. There is a short climb up to Hillhouse Farm, from where there are good views over the surrounding woods and fields. Follow the road downhill past Broomells Farm (nearly 24 miles) and around the sharp left-hand bend beyond. On the right is the open area of Misbrooks Green; if you come this way in summer, look out for the round purple-headed flowers of the Devil's-bit scabious, which grows here in profusion. Mizbrook Farm (note the variation in the spelling) is on the left, shortly before a bridge over a stream.

☞ *At the junction between Vicarage Lane and Temple Lane on the edge of Capel, you have a choice. If you wish, you can take a two-mile diversion along the turning on the left, a dead-end road leading to Temple Elfande. This house is said to have been built by the Knights Templar. It has a rectangular pond which may have once been a stew pond, used to keep the fish which were such an important element in the religious diet. (A new bridleway link has now been opened along the driveway of Temple Elfande.)*

On the way the peaceful lane passes Aldhurst Farm (like Mizbrook, it probably dates from about 1500), a large new property called Temple Mead, and some small cottages called Rushetts. At the latter, one of the residents has revived the craft of charcoal production, using locally-coppiced hornbeam and birch (☎ 01306 712850 for more information).

Return to the junction with Vicarage Lane and turn left in the direction of Capel. The lane, which is now quite built-up, comes out onto The Street opposite the church. Turn left, past the Crown, now the village's only pub, and continue along the road to the green at the far end (25 miles, or 27 with the diversion to Temple Elfande).

Ride E:
Gems of the Vale

Reigate Heath • Dungate's Farm • Buckland • Betchworth • Brockham • Box Hill Bridge • Dorking • Deepdene Estate • Brockhamhurst • Dawes Green • Leigh • Flanchford • Reigate Park • Reigate • Reigate Heath

Distance: 15½ miles
Landranger Maps: 187
Pathfinder Maps: 1206, 1207, 1226, 1227

Across much of Surrey, in the dip between the North Downs and the Greensand hills, is a band of highly fertile soil, enriched by chalk and sand washed down from the surrounding heights. To the west the band is narrow – sometimes little more than a field's width – but east of Dorking it broadens into the pretty Vale of Holmesdale.

Most people know the Vale only from travelling along the busy A25 and are unaware of the appealing villages which lie just off the main road. This ride passes through three of them – Buckland, Betchworth and Brockham – and along some delightful tracks and deserted lanes between them.

The ride is mostly easy going across level countryside. There are steep hills on the outskirts of Dorking and Reigate, but they are short and it's no great hardship to get off and walk for a few minutes. To compensate, there are some splendid views from the hilltops. In two places the ride emerges briefly onto the A25. You can walk on the pavement if you prefer not to cycle on this main road, although it's generally wide enough to ride out of the way of the traffic.

Starting Points

Start at the car park on Flanchford Road, a turning off the A25 just west of Reigate (grid reference TQ 238502), close to the windmill on Reigate Heath. There is also a large, secluded car park in the woods at Great Brockhamhurst (TQ 199470), to the south of Brockham and Strood Green.

⇌ The stations at Reigate, Betchworth (limited service), and Dorking (Deepdene) are all on Thames Trains' Reading–Guildford–Redhill–Gatwick line, while Dorking station is served by frequent trains from London – by South West Trains from Waterloo and Connex South Central from Victoria. All these stations are only a short distance from the route.

Ride E
Gems of the Vale

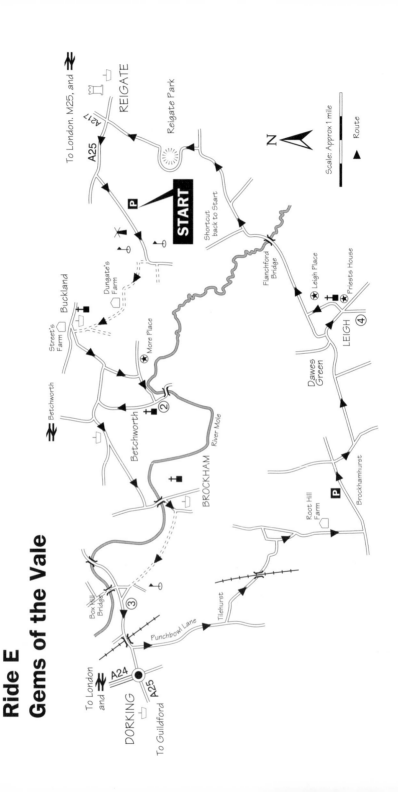

The Route in Brief

① Leave CP and head south away from A25. Halfway round sharp left bend, just before junction with Sandy Lane, TR onto unsigned track (BW). At oak tree bear round to L and then TL immediately before cottage. Continue on BW to Dungate's Farm, then onto tarred drive. At Pilgrim Cottage follow lane beside brick wall to reach Old Road. TL into Old Road, take next on L, Sandy Lane. At TJ at end TR into Wonham Lane.

② At Betchworth TR into The Street. Beyond village TL into Old Reigate Road. Pass end of Station Road. At next junction TL into Kiln Lane, SP Brockham & Newdigate. At end TL into Brockham Lane and cross bridge.

At the edge of village green TR into Old School Lane then TR just after Turners Bridge onto gravelled track of the old coach road of Betchworth Park (BW). Follow this until it joins drive to golf course. Go SO then take LF to reach A25.

③ TL onto A25. Immediately after railway bridge TL into Punchbowl Lane. Climb over hill then take next L, Tilehurst Lane, by group of cottages. Under railway then TR at next TJ, and R again, up Root Hill. TL at TJ into Brockhamhurst Road.

TR at XR, SP Leigh & Newdigate, then take next on L, SP Leigh. Keep SO past Dawes Green to Leigh.

√ TL by Plough pub into Church Road, SP Reigate. At TJ beyond Leigh Place TR, again SP Reigate. Cross Flanchford Bridge then continue SO into Clayhall Lane at next junction. At following junction TL into continuation of Clayhall Lane. About 350 yds after Clayhall Farm TL into Park Lane. Continue to edge of Reigate, junction with West Street (A25). TL into West Street and follow to Reigate Heath. TL into Flanchford Lane and return to CP.

The old coach road through Betchworth Park

Buckland Post Office

The Ride

① Reigate Heath to Betchworth

Leave the car park at Reigate Heath and head south (away from the A25). The windmill church (see page E12) is on the right, about a quarter of a mile along the road. After a gentle climb past a golf course there is a downhill run to a sharp left-hand bend. Halfway round the bend, turn right onto an unsigned track, just before the junction with Sandy Lane.

At the oak tree bear round to the left and then turn left immediately before the cottage. The track is sandy, but the surface is firm and you should have no problems. After a while it passes through a gate into a field, from where it continues straight ahead along a fairly obvious trail – a blue bridleway waymark indicates the correct direction. At the end of the field, pass through another gate and follow the track round to the left through a small copse.

The sound of running water comes from the Shag Brook, which flows under the track and forms a small pool on the right (1 mile). As you emerge from the trees there are huge beds of nettles along the bank of the stream, which, in summer, attract a host of butterflies.

From here the track is in excellent condition as it heads towards the farmyard of Dungate's Farm, a beautiful timber-framed red-brick house. Continue through the farmyard onto the tarred drive, which comes out by Pilgrim Cottage, then follow the lane to the right, along the side of a brick wall, to reach the Old Road by the Buckland Stores & Post Office. There is an interesting map of the parish in the bus shelter opposite.

Buckland *is cut in two by the A25 and, because of the notorious bends on the main road, motorists have to concentrate too much on their driving to appreciate the village scene. Not so cyclists.*

Just around the corner from the post office is the parish church, St Mary's, which was almost completely rebuilt in 1860, only the timber belfry surviving from its predecessor. Across the road is the village green with its pond and, beside it, a building which many passers-by mistake for a church – the black weatherboarded barn of Street's Farm with its unusual tower.

There may not be a great deal to see or do in this tiny village, but if you can forget the traffic, it's a lovely spot.

☐ *Buckland Stores & PO, 8.30–1, 2–6 (2.30–5 Sat; closed Wed pm and all Sun)*

Turn left into Old Road which, as its name implies, was the main road until the present A25 was built in the 1920s. At about the 2-mile point the road gently descends into the valley of a small stream. Just before the bottom, opposite some old stables, turn left into Sandy Lane, which climbs past the entrance to Hartsfield Manor (now a training centre for one of the banks), before ending at a junction with Wonham Lane. (The 15th century More Place is just to the left of the junction and is worth a diversion.)

Turn right into Wonham Lane, which soon bends to the left to run directly beside the river before emerging in the centre of Betchworth village, by the Dolphin pub.

Betchworth *developed at one of the few places where it's possible to cross the River Mole. The picturesque single-lane bridge, just south of the village on the road to Leigh, was built in*

Streets Farm, Buckland

Betchworth

1843 and is now protected by a weight limit, which also helps to keep heavy traffic out of the village.

Opposite the end of Wonham Lane is the entrance to Betchworth House, the clock tower of which can just be seen over the tall boundary wall. The house was originally built in 1634 but has been rebuilt and enlarged many times since then.

To the right of the house is St Michael's church, built mostly of grey firestone. It originally had a central tower which dated from Norman times, but in 1851 this was found to be unsafe and was demolished. It was replaced by the present tower, which occupies an off-centre position. During the work a fragment of carved stone from an earlier Saxon church was discovered and has now been incorporated in the south window. In the south transept is an ancient oak chest carved out of a single piece of wood.

Church Street is a complete contrast to long, narrow The Street. Turning the corner by the

Old Vicarage, the road opens into a delightful cul-de-sac with the church at the far end. On the left is a row of pretty cottages of varying ages, while on the right is a huge restored tithe barn, made of timber.

Back in The Street, opposite the end of Church Street, is the unusual Old House, its long 18th century facade masking a much older building.

The Dolphin, The Street. Youngs. 01737 842288. Food G

② Betchworth to Box Hill Bridge

Turn right out of Wonham Lane into The Street. After the junction with Church Street there is a gentle climb past the village school (3 miles) and along a winding stretch of road.

The Red Lion, Old Road. Friary Meux. 01737 843336. Food (not Sun eves) G

Turn left at the junction with the Old Reigate Road – the Red Lion pub is a short distance to the right – and continue past the end of Station Road, from where the road runs downhill past the local post office. When you get to the telephone exchange, a little further on, look across the fields to the left for a good view of the village nestling by the river. To the right are the downs, scarred by the quarries of the one-time Betchworth Lime Works.

At the next junction turn left into Kiln Lane, in the direction of 'Brockham & Newdigate'. The curiously-isolated estate of houses at Nutwood Avenue (4 miles) was built on the site of the Brockham brickworks, which closed in the 1920s. At the end of Kiln Lane, turn left into Brockham Lane and cross the single-lane Borough Bridge to reach the village.

Brockham *green badly needs a village cricket pitch to make it look complete. It used to have*

one until it was decided that the game posed too great a threat to the increasing number of parked and passing cars. The famous W G Grace once played there.

The church at Brockham wasn't built until 1847; before that, the village was part of Betchworth parish. The land for the church was given by the Lord of the Manor, Henry Hope of Betchworth Park, and the stone by Sir Benjamin Brodie of Broome Park, but the donated material was from Betchworth Quarry and it has worn badly, requiring some expensive repairs. The pump on the green was erected as a memorial to Henry Hope.

Perhaps the best place from which to view the green is by the church looking north. From there you can see how the village shelters under the lee of the Downs. Along the north side of the green are some pretty cottages and two pubs. Sandwiched incongruously between the latter is a Strict Baptist Chapel. The road that runs past the pubs leads to the gate of Brockham Court Farm, beside which is the

Cottages on the green at Brockham

small brick-walled village pound in which stray animals were once kept.

▦ *The Royal Oak, The Green. Free house. 01737 843241. Food C G*

▦ *The Dukes Head, The Green. Friary Meux. 01737 842023. Food C G Rest*

⊔ *Spar Grocers, Middle Street. Grocers, off licence, newsagents. Open 7.30–6.30 (to 7.30 Sat, 8.30–3.30 Sun)*

At the green, turn right (assuming you're facing towards the church) into Old School Lane, which heads downhill and over the small Turners Bridge. Just after the bridge turn right at the bridleway sign onto a gravelled track, the old coach road to Betchworth Park.

After passing a few houses, the track heads out across open farmland. Beyond the small pond on the left (5 miles), it passes through the old parkland, most of which is now a golf course. To the right, hidden in a copse, are the scant remains of the 14th century Betchworth Castle. It was partly taken down in 1690 and the remains incorporated in a house, which was itself demolished in 1837 when the park became part of the Deepdene estate.

When the coach road joins the golf course drive go straight ahead down the hill until the drive divides. To continue on the main route (see ③ below) take the left branch. To explore the old Box Hill Bridge, bear right, then cross the A25 into the dead-end road leading past the garden centre to an ugly steel footbridge. Look into the river on the right-hand side and you will see the remains of the old bridge piers beneath the surface. Look back along the other side and you can see the flood arches on which the long bridge approach was built.

Box Hill Bridge *carried the original, tortuous Dorking–Reigate road over the River Mole. As it left Dorking the old road followed what is now the approach to the golf course. A hairpin bend (at what is now the fork by the golf course*

entrance) then took it down towards the bridge. Having crossed the river, the road headed north towards Box Hill, the road to Reigate branching off to the right at a junction near Box Hill Farm.

In 1927 a new road (today's A25) was built through the riverside meadows which were part of Betchworth Park to bypass the sharp bends, and the old bridge became redundant. It lasted until 1968, when it was destroyed by floods.

Continue over the footbridge and up the gentle hill on the far side to the old junction where the roads to Reigate (to the right) and Box Hill parted company. An old cast-iron signpost, made in Dorking by Stone and Turner, stands by the junction, although, sadly, the arms have been broken off.

③ Box Hill Bridge to Leigh

From the golf course entrance turn left onto the A25 towards Dorking. The road is busy but broad, and you should be able to keep clear of the traffic – if you prefer, you can walk along this stretch.

Just along the road is the Watermill pub. The adjacent lane leads to the old Castle Mill (now a private home), from which the pub takes its name.

▦ *The Watermill, Reigate Road. Free house. 01306 887831. Open all day Food Patio Rest*

Cross the railway bridge (6 miles) and turn left into Punchbowl Lane, climbing steeply through the Greensand hills behind Dorking. This is one of the more affluent parts of the town, being developed during the 1920s and 30s out of part of the Deepdene Estate.

The Deepdene Estate *was once owned by the Howard family, through which descended the title of Duke of Norfolk. It was the tenth Duke who, between 1777 and 1786, built a grand Palladian-style house at Deepdene, but in 1807 the estate was sold to Thomas Hope, the son of a rich merchant.*

Hope was one of the first of the great 19th century collectors, as well as an enthusiastic amateur architect and designer. He soon set about planning alterations to the house, with the aim of creating what he called 'a picturesque effect' by combining classical and Italian styles in his designs and in the features of the surrounding gardens. The changes to the house were extensive and took more than 20 years to complete, being continued after his death in 1831 by his son, Henry.

The 20th century treated the magnificent mansion cruelly. After World War I it became a country hotel, becoming run-down and acquiring a dubious reputation. Much of the surrounding parkland was sold for development, and in 1933 it was decided to route the A24 Dorking bypass through the grounds, passing close to the front of the house.

In 1939 Deepdene was bought by the Southern Railway Company to allow its headquarters offices to be evacuated from London in the expected war. Caves in the grounds were used to house a control office and a telephone exchange, and the stable block was converted into 40 bedrooms. The Southern Railway kept the house after the end of the war, using it as its accounts department's office, and it passed into the ownership of British Railways after nationalisation in 1948. In 1969 it was sold to developers who demolished it and replaced it with offices.

A short downhill stretch leads to a small group of cottages at the junction of Tilehurst Lane (7 miles). Turn left here. The cottage, Tilehurst, on the corner is built of an unusual variety of materials, parts being timber-clad, stone-built and tile-hung.

Tilehurst Lane meanders peacefully through the fields and passes under the railway before reaching its junction with Parkpale Lane (8 miles), a name which commemorates the old boundary of Betchworth Park. Turn right here and, after two hundred yards, turn right again at a second junction, which is followed by the steady climb of Root Hill.

At the junction with Brockhamhurst Road (there was a cattle grid here until a few years ago) turn left and follow the road past Great Brockhamhurst (9 miles). The road is busier than the deserted lanes you have just left, so a little extra care is needed. A little further on the road passes Highridge Wood, where there is a car park.

At the following crossroads turn right in the direction of Leigh (pronounced Lie) and Newdigate. Once again, this can be a busy road at times, so ride with care. At the next junction turn left, following the sign for Leigh. Hook Cottage, a short way along the lane, marks the ride's 10-mile point. This is level Wealden countryside and for the next couple of miles the cycling is very gentle.

Continue past the junction by the cricket ground to reach Dawes Green. The pub there, the Seven Stars, has been skilfully renovated in recent years. Old extensions have been replaced by new construction more in keeping with the old, thanks to the use of materials recovered from demolished buildings. A photo display inside shows how it was done.

Also inside is a painted panel bearing a verse written in 1637 by the then landlord William Eades. It reads:

> Gentlemen, you are welcome
> To sit down at your ease
> Pay what you call for
> And drink what you please.

The Seven Stars. Friary Meux. 01306 611254. Open all day. Food C G

Follow the road through Dawes Green, past two turnings on the left, and continue to Leigh, passing the school (11 miles) as you approach the village.

Leigh *was once an important centre of iron-making in the Surrey Weald, but you'd hardly guess it from looking at this typical country village now. The heart of the village is its green, on which stands the picturesque covered well. Around it are clustered the church, the pub, and the Priests House.*

The church, which dates back to the 15th century, is unusual in having no aisles, and the bell-tower, added in 1890, and the lean-to porch combine to give it an odd, squat look. During the middle ages the village had no resident priest. Instead, a visiting priest was sent out from Newark Priory, near Woking, to which the manor belonged. The splendid medieval Priests House, facing onto the green, is said to have provided accommodation for these visits. Quite why Leigh retained this practice, one which was commonplace in Anglo-Saxon times, is not known.

The village pub, the Plough, mostly weatherboarded, completes the rural scene.

The Plough, Church Road. King & Barnes. 01306 611348. Food G Acc

√ **Leigh to Reigate Heath**

Turn left by the Plough into Church Road, signposted 'Reigate'. Keep an eye out for a couple of lovely cottages, on the left, just beyond the church. The lane bends to the left as it leaves the village and then, on the right, about 200 yards further on, it passes Leigh Place.

Leigh Place *occupies an old moated site which may date to the 12th century, but, although the bones of an ancient house may survive beneath its surface, what we see today dates from its rebuilding in 1810. Gothic with a dash of fairytale fantasy is perhaps the best way of describing it. In 1530 the estate was owned by Edward Shelley, an ancestor of the poet Percy Bysshe Shelley.*

At the T-junction after Leigh Place, turn right in the direction of Reigate. Pass Denshot Farm (12 miles) and the gates of Burys Court Prep School, and then cross the River Mole by the single-lane Flanchford Bridge. About 400 yards after this, when Flanchford Road turns off to the left, continue straight ahead along Clayhall Lane.

☞ *You can turn left at this junction to follow Flanchford Road back to the car park at Reigate Heath. This avoids the ride into Reigate and the short stretch of the A25 back to Reigate Heath.*

The lane climbs a little as it passes Flanchford Farm. At the next junction stay on Clayhall Lane as it branches off to the left. The countryside is open and deserted, strangely so, given that parts of Reigate are quite close by. The 13-mile point is passed before the first sign of habitation, Clayhall Farm, is reached. About 350 yards further on, opposite some modern houses, turn left into Park Lane. The road climbs steeply for almost half a mile, curving around the end of the sandstone ridge which is occupied at its western end by Reigate Park.

Reigate Park *was originally the deer park of Reigate Priory, established in 1235 by William de Warenne, the sixth Earl of Surrey. Its demise came at the Dissolution, 300 years*

later, when it was seized by the Crown and the estate was granted to William Howard, the first Lord Effingham, who built himself a house on the site. The present Priory, now a school, is late 18th century in style.

One of the most intriguing features of the Priory is the Tudor fireplace in the hall in the centre of the house. Made of stone, it has a carved oak surround which is so huge it was obviously never made for its present situation. Its origin is a puzzle – there are signs that it came from a royal house, but which one? The fabulous Nonsuch Palace, near Ewell, is one possibility but it had not been demolished when the diarist John Evelyn saw the fireplace at Reigate in 1655. He thought it came from Bletchingley Place, the house given to Anne of Cleves by Henry VIII (see ride H).

In the magnificent park, now an open space much enjoyed by local people, is the pond which once provided the monks with fish for their table. Nearby, on the top of the hill in the park, is a reservoir built in the mid-19th century to provide piped water to the town.

The climb eases at the junction with Littleton Lane (which offers another route back to Reigate Heath), from where there are superb views over the surrounding countryside.

As it rounds Park Hill, the road passes through a sandstone cutting (14 miles) emerging into the outskirts of Reigate. Watch for the splendid vintage shop front near the junction with West Street.

Reigate *owes its existence to the castle built by William de Warenne, Earl of Surrey, the son-in-law of William the Conqueror. Before then the only settlement was the Anglo-Saxon village of Cherchefelle, which was situated near the present parish church.*

Although the castle encouraged the development of a small town at the foot of its walls, its own history is undistinguished. Its 'decayed' remains, as they were described, were finally demolished by Parliamentary forces during the Civil War, to prevent it falling into

Royalist hands. Most of the rubble found its way into local buildings and roads, but a mock gateway, built in 1777, is said to have been built from some of the remains. Today the castle mound and its surrounding dry ditch (or fosse) is a public park, a peaceful green spot within yards of the High Street.

In the fosse is the entrance to the so-called Barons' Cave, cut into the sandstone which underlies the castle mound. The origins of the cave are unclear, but claims that it was the place where the barons met on their way to confront King John at Runnymede, which led to the signing of the Magna Carta, are no more than local invention. The cave is open to the public on occasional Saturdays during the summer.

Also cut through the castle mound is the road tunnel built in 1824 to carry traffic straight into the heart of the town. William Cobbett was furious at the waste this represented. "They are, in order to save a few hundred yards' length of road, cutting through a hill. They have lowered a little hill on the London side of Sutton. Thus is the money of the country actually thrown away; the produce of labour is taken from the industrious and given to the idlers." Cobbett was obviously one of the first road protesters.

Reigate is a pleasant town with a wide selection of shops, pubs, and other facilities, and is well worth spending some time in.

At the junction, turn left into West Street. (There are toilets opposite should you need them.) This junction was once the heart of Reigate, the triangular area formed by West Street, Upper West Street, and the delightful Slipshoe Street being the town's main market until the time of the Reformation, when it moved to the other end of the High Street.

West Street is the main A25 road and can be quite busy, but it is broad enough not to cause too many problems. Continue for just over half a mile to the junction with Flanchford Road (15 miles), and turn left.

The Black Horse, West Street. Friary Meux. 01737 245694. Food G

Pass the row of cottages facing onto the common, and continue for about 500 yards to the car park and the end of the ride, but before you leave, be sure to visit the famous Windmill church.

The Windmill Church, *built in 1765, is claimed to be the only building of its type in the world used in this way. It is a post mill with a brick base and a black weatherboarded tower. It was converted in 1865 and can, surprisingly, seat up to 50 people.*

Ride F:
Romans, Racehorses, and Writers

Burford Bridge • Fredley • Mickleham Downs • Tyrrell's Wood • Thirty Acre Barn • Langley Vale • Epsom Downs • Epsom • Tattenham Corner • Walton Downs • Headley • Burford Bridge • Westhumble • Ranmore Common • Polesden Lacey • Westhumble • Burford Bridge

Distance: 9 to 24 miles
Landranger Maps: 187
Pathfinder Maps: 1206, 1207, 1191 (corner only)

Romans, racehorses, and writers – a fascinating mixture of associations brought together on this ride. We begin our journey along the old Roman road, Stane Street, as it climbs out of the Mole Gap and makes its way over the downs towards Epsom. Today it is simply a rough track and the steep climb is hard work. At Thirty Acres Barn we leave the Roman road and make for Epsom Downs. From there, after venturing into the town, the route crosses the world-famous racecourse to Walton Downs. It then returns along country lanes and tracks through Headley to Mickleham and Burford Bridge, a corner of Surrey with a host of literary associations.

Crossing the A24, the ride passes through Westhumble, with its chapel ruins, and climbs the steep lane to Ranmore Common. From there a bridleway leads through the grounds of the National Trust property of Polesden Lacey and back onto the lane to Burford Bridge. This ride involves substantial climbs through the Downs, many of them steep, and is not for the inexperienced. Indeed, it is the most demanding in this book, but you can split it into two if you wish.

Starting Points

The best place to start is at the free car park by the roundabout on the A24 at Burford Bridge (grid reference TQ 171519), just north of Dorking, where there are toilets and a café. However, it can become very crowded at peak times.

There are large car parks near the racecourse on Epsom Downs (not on race days), on Ranmore Common (National Trust – pay and display), and two smaller ones on the lane between Headley and Mickleham (both free but a donation to the NT welcome).

⇌ Boxhill & Westhumble station, served by Connex South Central trains on the Victoria–Dorking line, is on the ride. There are connections at Epsom or Leatherhead if you are travelling from Waterloo, Guildford, or West Croydon. Epsom and Tattenham Corner stations are only a short distance from the ride.

Ride F
Romans, Racehorses,
and Writers

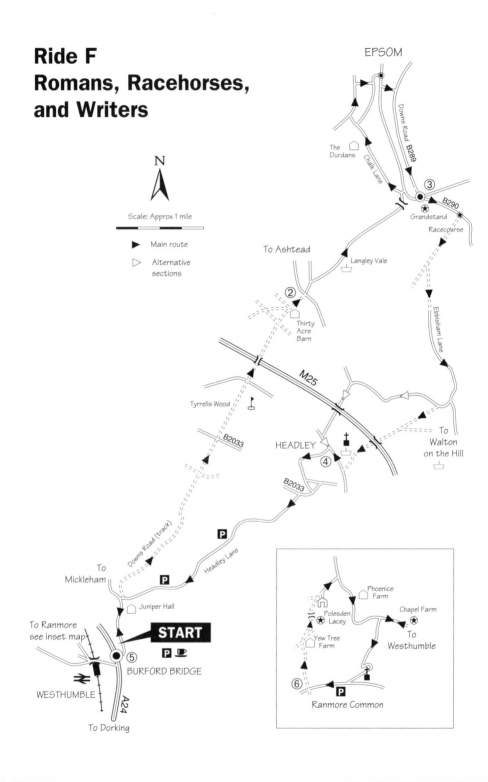

N

Scale: Approx 1 mile

► Main route

▷ Alternative
   sections

EPSOM

Downs Road B289

The Durdans

Chalk Lane

③ B290

Grandstand

Racecourse

To Ashtead

Langley Vale

Ebbisham Lane

②

Thirty
Acre
Barn

M25

Tyrrells Wood

B2033

HEADLEY

④

To
Walton
on the Hill

B2033

P

P

Downs Road (track)

Headley Lane

To
Mickleham

Juniper Hall

To Ranmore
see inset map

START

P

⑤

BURFORD BRIDGE

WESTHUMBLE

A24

To Dorking

Phoenice
Farm

Polesden
Lacey

Chapel Farm

Yew Tree
Farm

To
Westhumble

⑥

P

Ranmore Common

The Route in Brief

① TL out of the CP. After half a mile, just beyond Juniper Hall, TR into Headley Lane, then immediately L onto Downs Road (BY) which starts between entrance to Juniper Hill and electricity sub-station. Follow signs to Thirty Acre Barn as track crosses downs, then continue SO when it becomes Stane Street.

② Continue from Thirty Acre Barn to main road, then SO into Downs Road and through Langley Vale towards racecourse grandstand. Just after underpass TL into Chalk Lane (before traffic lights) and continue to TJ with Woodcote Road.

TR then R again into Avenue Road. At far end follow bend to L, then TR at mini-roundabout. Take next on L, Downs Hill Road, then R into Downs Road to reach roundabout by grandstand.

③ TL at Derby Arms roundabout B290, SP Tadworth. At next roundabout by Tattenham Corner pub, TR onto BW which crosses racecourse. Continue on BW for 250 yds beyond far side, then TL at junction of tracks, Cross gallops on Walton Downs and continue into Ebbisham Lane. Follow this to junction with Hurst Road. TR then TL onto first BW; follow this under motorway and up slope to Headley village. At end TR into Church Lane.

√ Beyond Cock Horse pub TL into Slough Lane. FR when lane divides after Dove Cottage, then TR at TJ with B2033. After 200 yds TL into Lodgebottom Road, SP Mickleham & Dorking. Follow lane to TJ with Old London Road, then TL for Burford Bridge.

⑤ At roundabout with A24 TL along cycleway, then walk bike through subway under main road. At far side take L exit then TR into Westhumble Street. Pass station entrance and over bridge. Pass Chapel Farm, then take next L turn. Continue uphill onto Downs. At TJ after Ranmore church TR, SP Guildford & Effingham.

≈ Opposite sign for Dorking Scout Council – Ranmore Campsite TR onto BW. Follow this until it merges with broader track then bear L. At Yew Tree Farm bear L onto tarred farm road, then FL when BW (signed) diverges from farm road. Cross yew-lined embankment then continue SO through walled cutting and under bridge. At gateway into Home Farm continue SO onto flint track. Pass turning to Goldstone Farm then join main drive of Polesden Lacey. Continue to road.

TR onto narrow lane and continue SO past Chapel Farm and Westhumble, retracing outward route back to Burford Bridge.

The Ride

① Burford Bridge to Thirty Acre Barn

Leave the car park and turn left into the Old London Road, heading away from the main road. Pass the turning to Box Hill, climbing steadily. Just beyond Juniper Hall, turn right into the unsignposted Headley Lane, and then turn left immediately onto the byway which starts between the gravelled entrance to Juniper Hill and an electricity sub-station. This is the Downs Road, a track running beside the Roman Stane Street (see panel). The actual Roman road is on the right of the track – the sub-station stands on its line.

(*Note*: there are plans to create a more formal entrance to Juniper Hill but this should not affect access to the Downs Road or make it more difficult to find.)

Much of the track is rough and climbs steeply, so it can be arduous. Watch out for mountain bikers hurtling down the other way, some of them only just in control. The surface is partly clay with flints and can be slippery in the wet.

The track passes through a cutting with trees on either side and then bends to the right past the mansion of Juniper Hill. As you climb higher there are remnants of an old fence on either side and at 1 mile you pass through an old iron gate and onto a more open, scrub-covered area of downland, by which point the track has joined the course of the Roman road. Follow the red byway waymark pointing straight ahead.

You are now on Mickleham Downs, owned by the National Trust. After about 300 yards watch out for a track which branches off to the right through a barrier. It leads to the open crest of the Down, from where there are some magnificent views to reward the short diversion.

The next part of the track runs along a terraceway cut into the side of the hill before turning sharp left around the head of a deep valley. (Follow the sign for Thirty Acres Barn.) It then climbs, and bends to the right to join the main alignment of Stane Street heading directly towards London.

For the next half-mile the way is generally flat, but there are one or two steep undulations where there was no easy way of avoiding dips in the ground, so the Roman road takes them in its stride. Some of the stones in the surface on this stretch are beach pebbles and it's believed they are part of the original road material, suggesting it was built northwards from the coast.

After crossing the bridleway from Givons Grove to Mill Way (2 miles) the landscape levels out, and there are good views towards London. The shape of the raised embankment or *aggar* on which the road ran is plainly visible along this stretch, especially if you view it from the field on the left. On the right of the track is part of Tyrrell's Wood golf course. After a few hundred yards comes a sharp downhill slope. Beware, because the track crosses the busy B2033 road at the bottom, so be ready to stop.

On the far side of the road the track becomes a bridleway and is barred to cars and motorcycles. A little way further on, at Rose Cottage, the track crosses the drive leading to the golf course club house, and becomes Pebble Lane.

Keep straight on when you come to Headley Road (3 miles), just beyond which is the bridge carrying Stane Street over the M25. As you cross the bridge it's amazing to think that 2,000 years ago the insignificant track you are cycling on was

Stane Street

A feat of Roman engineering

Of the Romans' many amazing achievements, the network of roads which they built across the country must be among the most outstanding. Stane Street, the road linking London to Chichester – the Roman city of *Noviomagus* – is an excellent illustration of the skills which went into planning these roads and the way they were built.

Perhaps the most remarkable feature of Stane Street is that as it leaves London it heads directly for the east gate of Chichester, nearly 60 miles away. No-one knows how the Romans achieved this feat of accuracy, since, as far as we know, they had no maps or compasses, and certainly no theodolites.

Roman roads were built in straight sections – we call them alignments – which could be anything from many miles to a few yards in length. When a Roman road had to curve, it did so by a series of short straight alignments. Tradition has it that Roman roads were invariably dead straight, but this is far from true. Stane Street demonstrates this very clearly, as you'll discover on this ride.

The Romans had an excellent knowledge of the countryside through which they built their roads, and Stane Street has several examples of places where they adapted the route to take advantage of natural features or overcome problems. At Ewell, for instance, they diverted the road onto a line parallel to, but 850 yards east of, the line it followed out of London. This diversion shifted the road off the sticky London clay and onto the dry chalk of the downs 3 miles sooner than would otherwise have been the case.

Further south there was a more difficult problem to overcome. Had the road followed the direct line from London to Chichester, it would have involved a steep descent into the valley of the River Mole and a difficult passage through the Leith Hill range. To avoid this problem the Roman surveyors diverted the road from Mickleham Downs onto a much easier route into the valley. Because this stretch is far from straight, it's not always obvious that it is a Roman road. In one place it winds around the head of a valley into which it would otherwise have had to dip.

The part of Stane Street which the ride follows is generally well preserved, and its construction – including the raised bank (or *aggar*) which carried the road – is easily recognised in many places along the way.

For more information on local Roman roads, see *Roman Ways in the Weald* by I D Margary, published by Phoenix House (3rd Edition 1965).

as important a traffic artery to the Romans as the motorway below you is to our age!

After a staggered crossways with another bridleway the track abandons the course of Stane Street and curves gently to the right to Thirty Acre Barn.

The bend is so slight you may not even notice it. It caused problems for the 19th century antiquarians who first tried to trace the course of the Roman road. They thought that perhaps Stane Street curved to the right here to head across Epsom Downs in the direction of Croydon.

It was only in the 1930s that the renowned archaeologist S E Winbolt excavated in a field just to the west of Thirty Acre Barn and discovered the remains of the road, proving that it continued on a direct line to London.

② Thirty Acre Barn to Epsom Downs

From Thirty Acre Barn follow the tarred road, Shepherds Walk, past some stables until you come to the road (4 miles). Go straight across into Downs Road, which is signposted 'Langley Vale & Epsom', and pass the junction with Headley Road, following the sign for 'Epsom Downs'. The road dips down to Langley Vale, where there are a couple of small shops, then climbs up onto Epsom Downs, with the racecourse on the right (5 miles). Take special care on this stretch – the road isn't too wide and the traffic can be busy. An underpass takes the road under the final length of the racecourse, past the Rubbing House pub.

The Rubbing House, Langley Vale Road. 01372 723245 Food

Stane Street, on the Downs near Epsom

The next part of the ride loops off the Downs into the outskirts of Epsom. The outward leg is attractive and interesting, but the return is mostly along suburban roads. If you'd rather omit this loop, turn right at the traffic lights along the B290, and rejoin the main route at the Derby Arms roundabout.

Immediately before the traffic lights turn left into Chalk Lane, an ideal, traffic-free route leading from the Downs almost to the centre of Epsom, passing the entrance to The Durdans (6 miles) on the way.

The Durdans *was once the home of the Earl of Rosebery, who succeeded Gladstone as Liberal Prime Minister in 1894, but resigned the following year. After that he abandoned politics and concentrated on racehorses until his death in 1929. Three of his horses won the Derby – Ladas in 1894, Sir Visto in 1895, and Cicero in 1905.*

The magnificent house was built in the 1760s, some of the materials being obtained, it's said, when the fabulous Nonsuch Palace at Ewell was demolished. The splendid wrought iron gates and cast iron piers of the entrance in Chalk Lane came from Canons, the Middlesex home of the Duke of Chandos.

Durdan's historical links include the fact that it's built on the course of Stane Street. If you look carefully at the brow of the hill in the field opposite the gates, you may be able to see a slight 'dent' which marks the continuation of its route.

Don't be surprised if you encounter a pack of police dogs enjoying a walk along Chalk Lane. There is a training establishment nearby and the road is a quiet way for them to reach the open Downs. Beyond The Durdans is a conservation area which continues to the junction with Woodcote Road. Many of the buildings proudly display plaques denoting that they are of historic interest. Not surprisingly, the local pubs are both named after famous racehorses. Amato won the Derby, the

only race he ever ran in, in 1838. He died six months later.

The Amato, Chalk Lane. 01372 721085. Friary Meux. Open all day Sat. Food G

The Ladas, Woodcote Road. 01372 723780. Charringtons. Open all day. Food 12–7 (exc Tue & Sat 12–2) G

The next part of the ride is along Woodcote Road, which is not ideal for cycling. If you wish, you can walk your bike along Madans Walk, which links the Ladas pub with Avenue Road.

Turn right into Woodcote Road, then take the next turning on the right, Avenue Road. Madans Walk comes out part of the way along this suburban street. Continue to the end of the road and follow it round to the left as it joins Worple Road. This leads to a mini-roundabout on Ashley Road, the B290.

For the town centre and its facilities, including pubs, shops, banks, toilets, and station, turn left into Ashley Road.

Turn right at the mini-roundabout and then take the first turning on the left, Downshill Road, which climbs steeply. At the top turn right into Downs Road, the B289 (almost 7 miles). Beyond the cemetery the road leaves the suburbs and emerges onto the Downs once more. There are some good views towards London and Docklands from these heights. Continue to the roundabout by the Derby Arms pub.

The Derby Arms, Woodcote Road, Epsom. 01372 722330. Toby Restaurants. Open all day. Food all day Rest G C

Epsom Downs *have been used for horse-racing since the 17th century, but its status was established in 1779 when Lord Derby instituted the Oaks, named after his downland house. The Derby followed a year later after Lord Derby and his friend Lord Rosebery tossed a coin to determine whose name should be attached to the world's premier Flat race.*

Waiting for a winner!

Derby Day brings thousands out onto the Downs to enjoy the spectacle. The first grandstand was built in 1829 and recent developments have seen the completion of the magnificent new Queen's Stand.

For information on Open Days and other special events ☎ 01372 726311.

③ Epsom Downs to Headley

From the Derby Arms roundabout take the B290 Tadworth road. There are some toilets about 350 yards along the road (8 miles). At the next roundabout, by the huge Tattenham Corner pub, turn right onto the bridleway which runs straight across the racecourse.

▦ *The Tattenham Corner, Tattenham Corner Road. 01737 351454. Beefeater. Open all day. Food Rest G C*

The bridleway is a public right of way, and you can cross the course even on race days, though you'll need to wait until the horses have passed by if you arrive while a race is underway.

At the far side of the course, continue along the bridleway for about 250 yards as far as a junction of tracks and then turn left. This track leads over the crest of Walton Downs (9 miles) and down the other side, crossing some gallops. Be careful because the tarred track is often covered with deep layers of wood chips or sand where these gallops cross.

The track eventually leaves the open Down and becomes Ebbisham Lane. At the start of the lane is an illegal rubbish dump. It may not be very attractive, but it's fascinating to see how many species of wildflower have managed to colonise such an inhospitable spot.

The lane is a bit rough at first, but it improves beyond the turning to Downs

View Farm. Shortly after the Wildwoods Riding Centre (10 miles) the lane ends at the triangular junction with Hurst Road. Turn right, then turn left at the next farm gate opening (signed Mid-Surrey Pony Club) onto a bridleway.

☞ *Part of this bridleway has a clay surface and it could be sticky and slippery after wet weather. If you would rather avoid it, see the alternative route on page 98.*

As you make your way down the bridleway you can see the spire of Headley church ahead. Keep straight on when a path comes in from the left, and climb towards the M25 which you can see just ahead. Go under the motorway (11 miles) and through an area of mixed woodland beyond. Keep straight on up the hill heading towards some houses, with Headley church to the right. The bridleway finally reaches the top of the hill and emerges onto Church Lane. Turn right and pass the Village Hall Stores, just outside which is a noticeboard with a map of the parish. The church is just ahead, tucked away behind the pub.

Headley's present church, the spire of which has served as a landmark on the ride for several miles, was not built until the 1850s. It replaced a medieval building which was, so it's said, in a ruinous state. The outline of the old church walls are marked by clipped yews, and some of its remnants were used to build the strange grotto-like structure in the churchyard.

🍴 *The Cock Horse (previously The Cock), Church Lane. 01372 377258. Ind Coope (Big Steak pub). Open all day. Food (all day) Rest C*

🏪 *Village Hall Stores, Church Lane. Post office and off-licence.*

√ Headley to Burford Bridge

Just beyond the pub turn left into the narrow Slough Lane, which heads downhill past a farm on the right which

keeps a variety of exotic fowl. Beyond a small turning on the right the lane becomes Tumber Street and reaches the bottom of the dip at Dove Cottage (12 miles). Take the right fork when the road divides immediately after this.

At the T-junction with the B2033, just opposite the track leading onto National Trust's Headley Heath, turn right. Watch out for the traffic. After about 200 yards, before the bottom of the hill, turn left into Lodgebottom Road, signposted 'Mickleham & Dorking'. Pause just after turning to admire the vista along the near-deserted chalkland valley through which the lane winds.

In the distance, on the top of the heights above Dorking, is the spire of Ranmore church – the destination of the next stage of the ride! For the time being, though, enjoy bowling along through the scenery. There's a small National Trust car park at Cockshot Wood (just over 13 miles) on the way down, and another at White Hill, a little further on. Beyond the second car park the left side of the road is lined by the flint wall of White Hill Cottage. This is followed by the junction with the Old London Road at Mickleham, which marks the end of the first loop of the ride. Turn left at the junction, past Juniper Hall, to return to Burford Bridge (15 miles). (Alternatively, turn right to visit Mickleham village, with its pub, *The Running Horses*. As you pass the churchyard, look out for the unusual lengthwise wooden graveboards.)

Box Hill has long been one of southern England's most famous beauty spots. As far back as the 18th century, when Epsom was at the height of its fame as a place to take the waters, it offered a pleasant excursion while waiting for the salts to have their effect! This popularity means that Box Hill, which is now owned by the National Trust, tends to become overcrowded at times. Surrey County Council

Juniper Hall
and the story of Fanny Burney

In 1792 a group of French aristocrats fled to England to escape the Revolution and the threat of its guillotine and made their home at Juniper Hall. Among their number were Mme de Staël, the Comte de Narbonne, Talleyrand – later to be French foreign minister – and General Alexandre d'Arblay.

It was at Juniper Hall in the January of 1793 that the novelist Fanny Burney met d'Arblay. They fell in love and, although her father was concerned that she had become, as he wrote, "entangled in a wild and romantic attachment which offers nothing in prospect but poverty and distress, with future inconvenience and unhappiness", they married in the August of that year.

Fanny Burney had a strange career as a writer. Her first book, Evelina, published in 1778 when she was 26, received critical acclaim, but it earned her just £30. The second, Cecilia, followed in 1782, and although it was thought to be not as good, brought her £250. Then, after her marriage, she wrote Camilla which, despite being rated by many as a decline from her earlier works, earned her no less than £2000 in the month of its publication! The fresh writing of the younger woman gave way, it seems, to the stilted, formal English of the Georgian era.

From the proceeds of this final book the d'Arblays built a cottage in the village of Westhumble which they called, appropriately, Camilla Cottage (see page 95).

Juniper Hall was later owned by Thomas Broadwood, the piano-maker, and eventually passed into the ownership of the National Trust, although it's not open to the public. Today it's used as a Field Studies Centre.

The course of the Roman Stane Street runs under Juniper Hall Lodge and through the garden. Part of its surface was revealed there many years ago when the lawns were being laid.

Almost opposite Juniper Hall is Fredley Manor, which, from 1797 to 1835, was the home of one Richard Sharp, a hat-maker, poet and member of Parliament,. He rejoiced in the nickname of 'Conversation' Sharp, thanks to his supreme skills in that art, and was visited at Fredley by most of the leading lights in the worlds of the arts and politics, including Wordsworth, Coleridge, and Macaulay. Of him Macaulay wrote "One thing I have observed in Sharp, which is quite peculiar to him among town-wits and diners-out. He never talks scandal. If he can say nothing good of a man, he holds his tongue."

is trying to tempt visitors to other parts of the Surrey Hills, but still the crowds come on sunny, summer weekends.

The hill takes its name from the box trees which flourish on the chalk there. At one time they were regularly harvested for their wood. On the summit is a stone marking the grave of the eccentric Major Peter Labillière of Dorking, who chose to be buried upside down. He argued that as the world was turned topsy turvy, he might come right at last. His request was granted when he died in 1800.

At the foot of Zigzag Hill is Flint Cottage, for long the home of poet and novelist George Meredith, who died there in 1909. He lived in simple fashion, climbing the hill early each morning, no doubt to fill him with inspiration. Many leading writers of the day, including Rudyard Kipling, J M Barrie, Robert Louis Stevenson, and Henry James, visited him there.

The hotel at Burford Bridge was originally a small inn known as the Fox and Hounds. Keats stayed there in 1818, also seeking the inspiration of a change of scene and air to put the final touches to his poem Endymion. Admiral Lord Nelson was another visitor, but probably not, despite local claims, on his final, fatal journey to Portsmouth and Trafalgar.

The hotel was largely rebuilt during the 1930s, when a magnificent 17th century tithe barn from Abinger was dismantled and re-erected there as a banqueting hall. Unfortunately, it's not open to the public.

⑤ Burford Bridge to Ranmore Common

Pass the Burford Bridge Hotel and, at the roundabout at the A24, turn left onto the cycle track alongside the main road, then dismount and walk through the subway under the dual carriageway. At the far side follow the ramp up to the left, then turn right into Westhumble Street.

▥ The Stepping Stones, Westhumble Street. 01306 889932. Friary Meux. Open all day. Food (all day) Rest G C (in Rest and G)

On the right just after the pub is the Royal School of Church Music in Cleveland Lodge. Continue along the road past the station entrance and over the bridge, where the road becomes Chapel Lane.

🚲 Action Packs Cycle Emporium, Station Approach. 01306 886944. Cycle sales, hire, service and repairs, maps, food

Camilla Lacey: The ornate flint arch inscribed Leladene on the right of Chapel Lane leads into the private estate which has been built on the site of Camilla Cottage, the home built by the d'Arblays (see opposite) on land given to them by their great friend William Locke, the owner of Norbury Park.

The cottage was built in 1797 and the d'Arblays lived in it for the next four years. Then, during a spell of peace between England and France, the general returned to his homeland with his wife and son. But the peace was short-lived and they were trapped in France until the war ended in 1815.

They returned to find that their friend and benefactor William Locke had died. His son, who had inherited the estate but not, it seems, his father's character, had discovered that, due to a technicality, the d'Arblays did not own the land on which Camilla Cottage stood. He forced them to sell him the cottage at a fraction of its cost.

Over the next 100 years the cottage was considerably extended. In 1906 it was inherited by Frederick Leverton Harris, a lover of art and literature, who converted two of the rooms into a small Burney museum. Tragically, a fire in 1919 destroyed the house and most of its contents. The distraught Leverton Harris sold the estate and a Tudor-style mansion was built in its place. In 1922 the estate was bought by an American, Victor Freeman. When his wife Lela died the following year he renamed the property Leladene in her honour.

Freeman was found dead in his bath in 1931 and in the following year, at the height of the Depression, the estate was sold. The Tudor *mansion was divided in two (literally by cutting through the centre of the building) and the present estate was built on the parkland on either side of Chapel Lane.*

From the railway bridge continue along Chapel Lane, past the chapel ruins and Chapel Farm. The 16-mile mark is passed at the junction with Burney Road.

Westhumble: *The small village clusters around the railway station, although its centre was probably once nearer the old ruined chapel. This was built in the 12th century as a chapel-of-ease, intended to save villagers a three-mile trek to the parish church in Mickleham, a difficult journey when the River Mole was in flood. It became derelict about 300 years later. In 1937 the ruins were handed over to the National Trust, in whose care they remain.*

Almost opposite the chapel is Chapel Farm, a working farm which was previously open to the public. However, the owners have now retired. The National Trust has acquired the farmland, but the farmhouse and its out-buildings remain in private ownership.

Further along Chapel Lane, just before its junction with Ranmore Lane, are the Westhumble Caves. The 'caves' are, in fact, a chalk quarry, which dates from the Middle Ages. It covers almost 2,000 square yards and is now sealed up to prevent access and accidents. It is a protected habitat for bats.

Leave the village heading up the valley, but then take the next turning on the left, Ranmore Common Road. It's marked by a Surrey Cycleway sign but no other signpost. From the junction the lane begins to climb, ever more steeply, towards the downs. At the 17-mile mark the open valley begins to give way to more wooded hillsides. A little further up the lane is the small but delightful Keepers Cottage, built of flint and brick.

The climb soon becomes very steep, and about half a mile beyond Keepers Cottage the lane bends sharply to the left. At the top of the hill, by one of the lodges of the Denbies Estate, it turns to the right, and is joined by the North Downs Way. A welcome stretch of level riding follows, past St Barnabus' church at Ranmore, the so-called Church of the North Downs (just over 18 miles).

Continue past the church to the T-junction and then turn right in the direction of 'Guildford and Effingham'. There's a National Trust Pay & Display car park just after the junction.

≈ Ranmore Common to Burford Bridge

The road runs through a broad green swathe on the top of the Downs, with occasional houses and cottages dotted around. Unfortunately the views to the south are limited by extensive tree growth, and you'll have to pause and make your way onto the National Trust-owned hillside to enjoy them.

Continue for some distance beyond the car park. Shortly after a small dip in the road watch out for a sign for the "Dorking Scout Council – Ranmore Campsite" on the left. Turn right here onto a bridleway (19 miles).

The bridleway is a pleasant, if slightly bumpy, trackway through woodland. Keep straight on when you come to a waymark post, ignoring the permissive bridleway which goes off to the right. Shortly afterwards the track crosses another – go straight on again – and then merges into a broader one; bear left.

The track winds through the woods before passing through a gateway with blue waymark arrows on each post. On the far side it's surfaced with flints and pebbles as it heads gently downhill into more open scenery. As it emerges from the trees, there's a splendid view of Polesden Lacey

Chapel Farm, Westhumble

across the fields on the far side of the valley, beyond Yew Tree Farm. A little further on you'll find a bench on the left of the track, from where there are some marvellous views to the west.

At Yew Tree Farm (about 20 miles), another bridleway joins from behind on the left. Keep going, bearing to the left onto a tarred farm road. There are magnificent views both to the right and ahead towards Polesden Lacey gardens.

Shortly after Yew Tree Farm there's a fork where the bridleway (signed) diverges to the left off the farm road. The track begins as a rough one heading into a shallow valley, but then it suddenly runs onto an immense embankment lined with yew trees, climbing steeply. At the top continue straight ahead on a tarred road in a cutting which is crossed by a thatched bridge. The cutting was dug in 1861 to prevent the road being seen from the

house and the spoil was used to form the yew-lined embankment. At the far end of the cutting the track comes out by an open field – with good views to the north – and the tarred road goes through a gateway into Home Farm. The bridleway continues ahead as a flint track.

A little further on, at a junction of paths, keep going straight ahead, past the turning to Goldstone Farm. The arched lodge of Polesden Lacey (built as recently as 1958) can be seen to the right, and soon the bridleway joins the main drive to the house. To visit the house turn right here, otherwise continue along the drive to the road (just over 21 miles).

Polesden Lacey: *The present house, which is owned by the National Trust and serves as their regional headquarters for southern England, is by no means the first to stand on this idyllic spot. Its earliest known occupant was a medieval building which was replaced in*

1631. In 1804 it was bought by Sheridan, the playwright, who lived there until his death in 1816. He described it as "the nicest place, within a prudent distance of town, in England".

After Sheridan's death the estate was bought by Mr Joseph Bonsor, who had the house demolished in 1824 and an elegant Regency villa, designed by Thomas Cubitt, took its place. The house was extended by subsequent owners, notably the Hon Mrs Ronald Greville, the Edwardian hostess, who had it entirely remodelled in 1906. Many of the leading society and political figures of the day were entertained there, and the Duke and Duchess of York, later King George VI and Queen Elizabeth (the Queen Mother), spent part of their honeymoon there.

Mrs Greville died in 1942 and bequeathed the house, its contents and the surrounding estate to the National Trust in memory of her father. The grounds are open daily 11–6 (or dusk if earlier). The house is open Wed–Sun from Apr to Oct, 1.30–5.30, also BH Sun and Mon 11–5.30. (Separate entrance fees for house and grounds.) ☎ 01372 458203 or 452048 for further details.

At the end of the drive turn right onto the narrow lane. There's a gradual uphill climb which levels out at Phoenice Farm, shortly after which is a reservoir, from where you can see back to Ranmore Church, showing how far you've come. A 1-in-5 (20%) slope follows. It's very tempting to go headlong down the hill, but resist the urge a little because you'll want to be able to admire the magnificent view towards Box Hill. Bagden Farm, on the right, is at the 22-mile mark, from where the road runs down past the junction of the Ranmore Common lane, and then retraces your outward route past Chapel Farm and into Westhumble (23 miles). There's a slight uphill climb through the village, followed by a run back down to the main A24 road. Cross by the subway to return to the Burford Bridge car park (almost 24 miles).

Alternative section of route

③ Epsom Downs to Headley

☞ *This alternative avoids the bridleway between Hurst Road and Headley.*

Continue along Hurst Road for about a mile. At the T-junction with Hurst Lane, turn left for Headley and Leatherhead and pass under the motorway. At the entrance to Headley Park Farm follow the road round to the left. A long steady climb follows. At the T-junction by the forge turn left for Headley and Box Hill. The National Trust property of Oyster Hill is on the right. After about 300 yards turn right into Slough Lane and rejoin the main route. (Headley village is straight ahead.)

Ride G:
Downland Delights

Margery Wood • Lower Kingswood • Gatton • Merstham • Rockshaw •
Gravelly Hill • Whitehill • Chaldon • Farthing Down • Hooley • Banstead Heath
• Walton Heath • Mogador • Margery Wood

Distance:	20½ miles
Landranger Maps:	187
Pathfinder Maps:	1207

One of the joys of cycling is seeing some of the more delightful and unusual
places in the countryside which you'll never see from a car, and this ride,
which explores the beautiful downland countryside south of Banstead,
Coulsdon, and Caterham, illustrates the point to the full.

A parkland estate which was once one of the country's most notorious 'rotten
boroughs', churches with fascinating and unusual features, strange towers, a
tiny remnant of the world's first public railway, and a downland hilltop where
our Saxon ancestors buried their warrior leaders, are among the intriguing
sights you'll see.

The ride requires some energy. Although much of it is quite gentle, there are a
few strenuous climbs, balanced by some exhilarating downhill dashes. Most
of the off-road tracks are in good condition, although the stretch over Banstead
Heath can be hard going after wet weather, thanks to the many horses
exercised there.

Starting Points

Start at Margery Wood. There is a large
free National Trust car park at the end of
Margery Lane (grid reference TQ
245527). To reach it, turn left off the
A217 London–Reigate road just north of
its intersection with the M25 motorway at
junction 8. As an alternative, there is a
free car park on Farthing Down, south of
Coulsdon (TQ 301571), but remember
that it's locked promptly at dusk.

≷ The station at Merstham is only a
short distance from the ride. It is served by
Connex South Central trains on the
London–Gatwick–Brighton line. Coulsdon

South, on the same line, and Smitham, on
the branch from Purley to Tattenham
Corner, are only a mile or so north of
Farthing Down but more than 200 feet
below its crest. Caterham station,
terminus of another branch from Purley
can be reached from Gravelly Hill (see
stage ②).

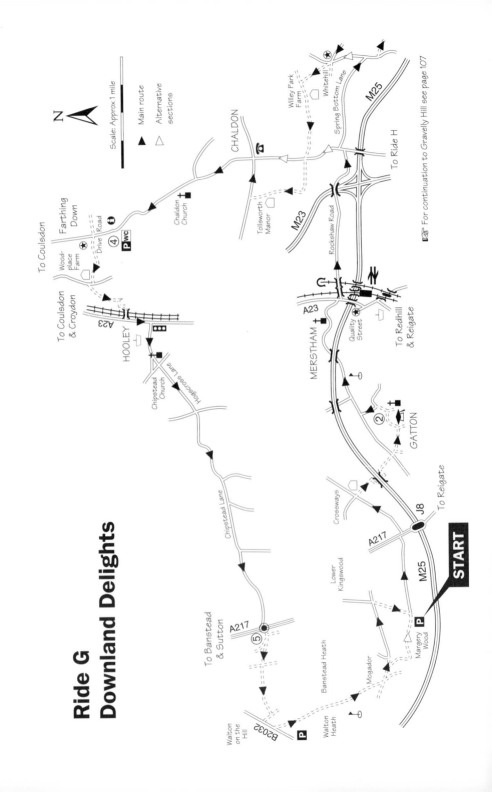

Ride G
Downland Delights

Scale: Approx 1 mile

N

▲ Main route
△ Alternative
  sections

To Coulsdon

Farthing
Down

CHALDON

Wood-
place
Farm

Drive Road

④ P wc

Chaldon
Church

Willey Park
Farm

Whitehill

Spring Bottom Lane

M25

To Ride H

To Coulsdon
& Croydon

A23

HOOLEY

Tollsworth
Manor

M23

Rockshaw Road

Chipstead Church

Hogscross Lane

A23

MERSTHAM

Quality Street

To Redhill
& Reigate

Chipstead Lane

GATTON

②

Crossways

J8

To Reigate

Lower
Kingswood

A217

M25

START

To Banstead
& Sutton

A217

⑤

Banstead Heath

Mogador

Margery Wood

P

Walton
on the
Hill

B2032

P

Walton
Heath

For continuation to Gravelly Hill see page 107

The Route in Brief

① From CP head east along Margery Lane. At the A217 cross over and TR, then TL into Blackhorse Lane. At the staggered crossroads by Crossways Farm TR into Crossways Lane, SP Bridleway. Continue along lane (becomes rough track at crest of hill) under motorway to road at bottom. Cross road into Gatton Park then FL along drive (BW). SO through gate the up slope past school buildings and playing fields. At school chapel ride continues to L, or take second on R to visit church.

② From school chapel follow drive onto road by North Lodge and TL. After 300 yds, TR into Gatton Bottom. Continue along road to junc with A23 and TR. Watch for traffic. To visit Merstham continue SO over motorway, otherwise TL into Rockshaw Road.

After 1 mile cross motorway near M23/M25 intersection. Continue to TJ at Warwick Wold Road. TL then almost immediately TR into Spring Bottom Lane, SP Caterham. At the far end TR into Whitehill Lane, SP Nutfield & Bletchingley. After 150 yds, just after SLOW sign, TL into Hextalls Lane (BW).

At crossways of tracks SO into Roughetts Lane. At gates of Roughetts follow BW to L between stone gateposts, then at junction in track take L branch. At next junc of paths TL onto broad track (only narrow footpath continues ahead). Go on for a few yds past junction of several minor paths to a main track. At next junc follow track to R, then continue until it emerges at Gravelly Hill picnic area.

③ Set off from picnic area in direction from which you arrived, but on road. At TJ with Whitehill Road go SO onto BW between gateposts of Willey Park Farm, then FR just inside. On approach to farm follow track to left, then keep SO past farm. At road continue SO onto BW

opposite. After 300 yds keep SO on main track when N Downs Way branches to L across sloping field, then follow it round sharp R bend. Continue to road past Tollsworth Manor and TR. At Chaldon XR TL into Church Lane. Keep SO to Farthing Down CP.

√ TL onto BW (Drive Road) immediately before gates and cattle grid. At Gate 2 continue down into valley and up far side to Woodplace Farm. Pass through yard to road and TR, then TL onto BW just before Star Shaw Stables. Follow BW round sharp bends to R, then L, then R again (over railway) to A23 road at Hooley. TL for 300 yds then R at traffic lights into Star Lane. Climb hill and follow bend to L, then FL past church. At XR continue SO into Hogcross Lane. SO at High Road into White Hill, SP Mugswell & Lower Kingswood. Pass Well House Inn and keep going to roundabout on A217, then SO to BW on far side.

⑤ Pass barrier onto Banstead Heath then FL when track divides. At next junction of paths TR then immediately L along edge of woods. Pass through gap in hedge then follow track as it veers to L past garden of house. At next junction take path SP Dorking Road 200 yds. TL along road for 100 yds then L just after bottom of dip onto BW along side of golf course.

At sign for permissive horse ride go SO, keeping to R of hedge. At next junction follow BW on left, SP Mogador ¼ mile. At next fork keep L to reach road – continue straight ahead. At next XR TR into Buckland Road past Mint Arms. Keep SO onto rough track to reach CP at Margery Wood.

The Ride

① Margery Wood to Gatton Park

Leave the car park and head east along Margery Lane. When you come to the A217, walk your bike across to the far side of the dual carriageway, turn right along the main road and then turn left into Blackhorse Lane after a few yards.

The stretch of the lane leading from the main road is broad, but it narrows suddenly and then you're in open country (1 mile). At the staggered crossroads turn right into Crossways Lane, signposted 'Bridleway', ignoring the no-through-road sign.

The lane passes Crossways Farm and climbs gently to the crest of the Downs, from where there are some wonderful views. Directly ahead is the ridge at Nutfield, with its fuller's earth factory (see Ride H). The lane is tarred this far, but the descent is on a rough track. At the bottom of the slope, the track diverts to the right to pass under the M25, resuming its original line on the far side of the motorway, from where it's only a short distance to the road.

Cross the road into the grounds of Gatton Park, ignoring the 'Private – No Through Road' sign at the entrance. Just inside take the left branch of the drive, which is signed as a bridleway (2 miles). (The right branch leads into a part of Gatton Park which is owned by the National Trust, and thereby to the top of Reigate Hill.)

The drive passes through a belt of woods, then through a gate and past an adventure playground. (This part of the park is now used as a school.) When the drive bends to the left a small lake called the Hop Garden Pond can be seen on the right but, sadly, the main lake cannot be seen from here. (The bridleway heading right from this point leads to the A242 between Redhill and Reigate.) Climb the slope past the modern school buildings and the sports fields. At the junction by the school chapel the ride continues to the left, but to visit St Andrew's church take the second on the right.

Gatton Park: In times long ago when kings of England were rulers and not simply figureheads, they needed parliaments which were ready to do their bidding. One way in which they achieved this was to grant the status of 'Borough' to the estates of trusted supporters. With this status went the right to elect members of parliament, and as most estates had only a few voters, in practice the MPs were simply appointed by the landowners. As a result of this dubious practice they became known as 'rotten' or 'pocket' boroughs.

Gatton was made a borough in 1451 by Henry VI as a reward for the services of his steward, John Tymperley. With it went the right to elect two MPs. (Only two years before this Tymperley had received the king's permission to turn Gatton into a park, so he must have been a royal favourite.)

Gatton passed through many ownerships over the years. In 1751 it was bought by Sir James Colebrooke, who employed Capability Brown to landscape the park and construct the 40-acre lake. His brother, George, built the 'Town Hall', a small open Doric temple, almost as a cynical monument to the corrupt political system.

In 1830 it was sold to the fifth Lord Monson, who paid the phenomenal sum of £100,000 for it. Two years later the Reform Act put paid to the rotten boroughs, but not before William Cobbett had described Gatton as 'a very rascally spot of earth'. Monson reconstructed the Hall on a grand scale and filled it with treasures acquired on his travels around Europe. He built the spectacular marble hall which, unfortunately, was totally ruined in a fire in 1934.

St Andrew's church, Gatton

He also refitted St Andrew's church with furnishings gathered from abroad. In style, the interior of the church resembles an Oxford or Cambridge college chapel, with rows of stalls facing each other across the nave. They came from a Benedictine monastery in Ghent, while the canopies above them were from Aürschot Cathedral in Louvain. The carvings on the pulpit are from Nuremburg and are attributed to the school of Albrecht Dürer.

The north transept is enclosed to form a family pew with chairs and a Victorian fireplace, more a lounge than a pew. The overall effect of the interior may not be to everyone's taste, but it should not be missed.

Lord Monson died at a very young age and is buried just outside the church. Also buried in the churchyard is a later owner of the hall, Jeremiah Colman, of mustard fame.

The church is open to the public during services and on Friday, Saturday and Sunday afternoons between April and September. The

rest of the park is the property of the Royal Alexandra and Albert School and, apart from the bridleways which pass through it, it's not open to the public.

② Gatton Park to Gravelly Hill

Follow the drive away from the school buildings and out onto the road by the North Lodge. Turn left and then, after 300 yards, turn right into Gatton Bottom.

This is an unclassified road, but it's used as a short-cut and can often be busy, so take care. It runs downhill parallel to the M25, past the junction with Markedge Lane (3 miles).

A little further on it bends left to pass under the motorway and then narrows, winding attractively at the foot of the hills as it approaches the village of Merstham.

The Surrey Iron Railway

The world's first public railway

In a small garden by the junction of Quality Street and Merstham High Street is a short section of track from the world's first public railway – the Surrey Iron Railway – which terminated only a few hundred yards from the spot.

The first ten-mile section of the railway, running parallel to the River Wandle between the Thames at Wandsworth and Croydon, opened in 1803. It had originally been intended to build a canal, but the owners of mills and factories along the river objected to the possible effect on its flow if its water was used to supply the canal.

A southwards extension of the railway, opened two years later and known as the Croydon, Merstham and Godstone railway, was originally planned as part of a scheme to reach Portsmouth. However, Nelson's victory at Trafalgar removed the threat to shipping in the Channel which had first spawned the idea, and the line never progressed beyond Merstham, where it served the Greystone Lime Quarries. The quarries can still be seen but they are now partly cut through by the later main line railway and, more recently, the M23 motorway.

The railway was open to the public on payment of a toll. Users provided their own horses and wagons. This was a revolutionary idea, for although canals were operated on a similar basis, all previous railways and wagonways in Britain had been built and worked as private lines, carrying minerals for their owners.

The Surrey Iron Railway used L-shaped iron 'edge' rails mounted on stone-block sleepers to guide ordinary flangeless wagon wheels. This allowed the wagons to be used on the roads as well as the railway.

However, the line belonged to an age that was fast passing as far as its technology was concerned. In 1839 a steam-worked railway opened between London and Croydon, and in 1841 it was extended to Brighton. The Croydon, Merstham and Godstone closed in 1838, its traffic already in decline. Part of its route was taken over by the new line to Brighton, but odd sections remain as footpaths. The rest of the line between Wandsworth and Croydon was abandoned in 1846.

Apart from the remains in Merstham, further relics of the railway can be seen in Guildford Museum, including the remains of a wagon used on the line, and observant passers-by along the route of the line may notice some of the stone sleepers which have survived in walls and rockeries.

Watch out on the left for Wellhead Cottage, with an unusual tower on the hillside above it, the first of several curious towers you will see on this ride.

Turn right when you come to the main A23 road, taking special care because of the traffic (4 miles). If you want to visit Merstham, continue along the main road over the M25, otherwise turn left into Rockshaw Road.

Merstham *was a small village at the foot of the downs on the London–Brighton road. It may have grown now, but it's still surprisingly pretty, considering that the A23 runs through the middle of it. The M23 may have taken away the through traffic, but plenty remains.*

The best feature of the village is Quality Street, a cul-de-sac which leads to the gates of Merstham House. It's named after the play by J M Barrie in which the actor Sir Seymour Hicks appeared during the time when he lived at The Old Forge at the end of the street. The

houses date from many different centuries, but they blend well and the overall effect is superb.

The main road bends sharply in the middle of the village, so that Quality Street looks as though it was supposed to be a continuation of the High Street. That was indeed the case until 1805, when the main road was diverted to the east along its present course.

Merstham is famous for the stone which was quarried locally, which was used in the construction of many buildings of national prominence, including Westminster Abbey, Windsor Castle, and the old London Bridge. It's said that in the west chancel arch of Merstham church is a piece of this bridge, a carving of a shield bearing three leopards, brought back to the village when the bridge was demolished. The stone, a grey chalk marl known as firestone for its ability to resist the effects of heat, can be seen in several buildings around the village.

There are a couple of pubs and a reasonable selection of shops.

Railway relics at Merstham

🖫 *Railway Arms, London Road North.*
Charringtons. 01737 642289. Food G
🖫 *The Feathers, High Street. Ind Coope*
01737 642498. Food (Big Steak pub) G C

Rockshaw Road crosses two successive railway bridges and then runs along a narrow ridge which proved attractive to Edwardian property developers, who built the substantial houses which line the road, sited to take advantage of the views.

Sadly, the valleys on either side of the ridge subsequently proved attractive to motorway builders, with the result that the ridge is now sandwiched between the M23 to the north and the M25 to the south. The road crosses the M23 by a long bridge, just north of its massive intersection with the M25 (5 miles).

The road eventually turns away from the motorway and comes to a junction with Warwick Wold Road. Note the old weight restriction notice, made of concrete, at the end of Rockshaw Road. It was made by the old Southern Railway, part of the prodigious output of its pre-cast concrete works at Exmouth Junction in Devon. Opposite the junction is the entrance to Rockshaw House, the lodge of which has an almost fairy-tale quality about it.

🖙 *To connect with Ride H, turn right into Warwick Wold Road and cross the motorway (again). Join the ride by turning left at the T-junction with Merstham Road.*

Turn left into Warwick Wold Road and then, after a brief climb, turn right into Spring Bottom Lane, in the direction of 'Caterham'.

🖙 *You can cut the ride short at this point by continuing up the hill past the junction with Spring Bottom Lane into Hilltop Lane.*

The scenery is once again rural, with the scarp slope of the Downs rearing up on the left. Further along the road there was once a massive chalk quarry. It's now mostly

returned to nature and overgrown, but houses have been built within it in a few places. At the end of Spring Bottom Lane (just over 6 miles) turn right into Whitehill Lane, signposted 'Nutfield & Bletchingley'.

🖙 *You can also cut the ride short here by turning left into Whitehill Lane, rejoining the route at the top of the steep hill.*

After 150 yards, just beyond the 'SLOW' sign, turn left into Hextalls Lane. Although it's signed as a private road, there's a bridleway sign just inside the turning. On the hilltop to the left at War Coppice is an Iron Age hillfort, unusual among Surrey's southern hillforts in being sited on the chalk hills rather than the Greensands.

When you come to a crossways of tracks carry straight on into Roughetts Lane. The track, now with a slightly rougher surface, descends a gentle slope. At the gates of Roughetts follow the bridleway as it veers to the left between two stone gateposts. This leads to a pleasant ride through woodland, climbing, but not too steeply. At a junction in the track (7 miles) take the left-hand branch, a dirt and gravel track along which the climb continues.

Indeed, the track steepens as it approaches a junction of paths. A broad path crosses from left to right, with only a narrow footpath continuing ahead. Turn left, then go on for a few yards past a junction of several minor paths until you come to a main track. At the next junction follow the track round to the right; note the oak symbol of the North Downs Way.

There is clay in the soil on this stretch and the surface may become sticky after wet weather. The track runs along a ledge cut into the steep hillside above the motorway, which can be heard a little too clearly for comfort if the wind is blowing from the south.

After a final climb the track emerges into the open space of Gravelly Hill, from where there are some magnificent views. A drinking water tap has also been thoughtfully provided by the local council (not in winter). This is an ideal place to rest for a picnic.

☞ *If you wish you can continue ahead along the road to reach Caterham. Keep heading downhill until you come to the Square in the centre of the town, then turn left past the station, and left again into Harestone Valley Road. Fork right at the church into a road which leads back uphill through a pleasant residential area and past Caterham School (where it becomes Weald Way) to War Coppice Road. Turn right to rejoin the main route.*

③ Gravelly Hill to Farthing Down

From the picnic area turn back in the direction from which you arrived, but stay on the road (War Coppice Road). There's a short climb and then, on the right, is an unusual battlemented water tower, built in 1862. A little further on, at the bottom of a steep dip, the junction with Weald Way marks the ride's 8-mile point.

There's another unusual tower on the right by the T-junction with Whitehill Lane. This one was built as a folly in about 1800 and is now completely derelict. The Harrow pub is about 100 yards to the right from the junction.

🍺 *The Harrow, Stanstead Road, Caterham. Friary Meux. 01883 343260. Open all day Mon–Sat. Food (exc Sun eve) G*

Go straight ahead at the junction, between the gateposts of Willey Park Farm, following the sign for the North Downs Way (the right-hand of the two tracks). There are some tremendous views along the line of the Downs from here, with Reigate Hill and Leith Hill visible to the west. From a little further along the tarred

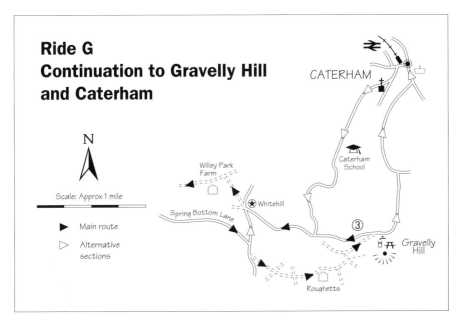

**Ride G
Continuation to Gravelly Hill and Caterham**

CATERHAM

N

Scale: Approx 1 mile

▶ Main route

▷ Alternative sections

Willey Park Farm

Whitehill

Spring Bottom Lane

Caterham School

③

Gravelly Hill

Roughetts

Farthing Down

farm track there are equally good views towards London, the Crystal Palace TV transmitter being prominent, and Canary Wharf just visible in the far distance.

The track bends to the left and merges with another, known as Pilgrim's Lane, as it approaches Willey Park Farm (about 9 miles). Immediately before the farm is a pond, next to which is a water tower built of flint and brick. Beyond the much-altered 17th century farmhouse is a granary built of similar materials.

The track becomes a little rougher from this point, but you shouldn't have any problems. Keep straight on, ignoring all side paths. Towards the end of the track there are occasional houses bordering it (just under 10 miles).

☞ *The track forks as it approaches the road. Take the left branch for the main route via Tollsworth Manor. However, this involves about half a mile of road which, while being unclassified and quite narrow, serves as a short-cut between Caterham and the A23. If you'd rather avoid this, take the right fork and turn right along Hilltop Lane to Chaldon crossroads.*

Cross the road into the continuation of the bridleway. After about 300 yards the track divides as the North Downs Way slopes off to the left across a field. Stay on the main track and follow it round a sharp right bend. There are good views from here, though motorways feature prominently.

The track leads past Tollsworth Manor, an extremely attractive farmhouse, mostly of the 16th century but with some even earlier parts.

Continue along the track until you come out on Rook Lane, then turn right. Take care because the lane bends and your view of on-coming traffic is limited.

At Chaldon crossroads, where there's a phone box, turn left into Church Lane (11 miles). (If you've come by the Hilltop Lane route, continue straight across the crossroads.) Chaldon church is outside the village, about half a mile along the narrow, winding lane.

Chaldon is a compact downland village just to the west of Caterham. Its small church is about half a mile outside the village on the lane to Farthing Down. It's remarkable for its wall painting, which dates from about 1200 and is said to be one of the most important examples of its age.

Wall paintings were common in churches in the Middle Ages. At a time when few people could read they provided graphic illustrations of religious themes, and many a medieval preacher found them useful as 'visual aids'!

The Chaldon wall painting, on the west wall of the church, combines the Last Judgement with the Ladder of Salvation. Set on a dark red ochre background, the painting is of the fire and brimstone tradition. It is divided into two tiers, of which the lower represents Hell and the upper Purgatory, with a ladder leading towards Heaven at the top, up which naked bodies scramble in search of salvation.

A postcard of the painting and an explanatory leaflet is available inside the church.

From the church continue northwards along the lane, now called Ditches Lane. A couple of hundred yards further on the lane enters Greater London, the left edge of the road being the county boundary. After a wooded stretch a small group of houses heralds the approach to Farthing Down, where there's a car park, public toilets, and information boards (just over 12½ miles). Refreshments are available from a mobile stall at busier times of the year.

Farthing Down is now owned by the Corporation of London, and has thus been saved from encroachment by suburbia which is all too obviously visible from the northern

end of the Down. The City's wealth has been put to good use in preserving open spaces around London since the 1870s. Epping Forest, Hampstead Heath, and Burnham Beeches are among the areas it has saved over the years, while Ashstead Common in Surrey is one of its latest acquisitions.

Farthing Down is rich in history. On the ridge are the remains of Iron Age or possibly Roman field systems. The later Saxon age is represented by a collection of barrows, originally some 30 in number, and the cemetery of which they formed part.

The barrows were the graves of the powerful and wealthy. In one of them was found the skeleton of a giant Dark Ages warrior, well over 6 feet tall, his sword lying across his body, and beside him an iron boss, which was all that remained of his wooden shield. Another barrow held the remains of a woman, with whom was found a wooden drinking cup, circled with bronze bands bearing a pattern of coiled snakes.

From the top of the down you can see two of the many hospitals and asylums that were built on these heights by the old London County Council in the last century. They reckoned the air would be beneficial to the patients' health. The nearest, almost hidden in the trees to the south west, is the Netherne Hospital; Cane Hill, at Coulsdon, is away to the north west. Their prominent water towers mark them out.

√ Farthing Down to Banstead Heath

The road across Farthing Down leads only to the suburban sprawl of Coulsdon in the valley below, so the ride turns off onto Drive Road on the left just before the cattle grid. It's marked by blue-topped posts signifying a bridleway. (If you wish you can explore the Down and then return to this point to continue the ride.)

The bridleway is mainly used by horses and is a soft dirt track. When you get to the junction at Gate 2 continue straight on down the hill into the valley and up the other side (13 miles). At the top of the climb is Woodplace Farm, where you are likely to be greeted by an old London Transport bus; some of the farm buildings are used for storing vintage commercial and military vehicles.

Follow the track straight through the farmyard. When you come to the road turn right for a short distance and then turn left onto another bridleway beside the entrance to Star Shaw Stables. It leads into the valley, which is occupied by both the London–Brighton railway and the A23 road.

Some way down the hill the bridleway turns sharp right, passes in front of a modern house, then turns left along a fence. After a final turn to the right it crosses twin bridges over the railway before reaching the main road at Hooley.

Turn left at the main road and continue for about 300 yards – if you find the traffic daunting you may prefer to walk along this stretch – then turn right into Star Lane at the traffic lights by the petrol station (just over 14 miles). There's a steep but relatively short climb out of the valley. At the top follow the bend to the left and then, just beyond the entrance to Court Lodge, fork left past the impressive, solid-looking 13th century church.

The church does not belong to Hooley, but is, in fact, the parish church of Chipstead, set a good mile from the village it serves. The monument beneath the tree on the green describes how it was planted in November 1945 to replace one destroyed during the war.

At the crossroads continue straight across into Hogscross Lane. There's an easy climb up to Noke Farm, from where the road runs gently downhill. Cross High Road (15 miles) into White Hill, which is

signposted to 'Mugswell & Lower Kingswood', descending rapidly into a tranquil and near-deserted valley. It's astonishing that this isolated spot survives so close to roaring roads and bustling suburbia.

The splendidly-named Pigeonhouse Lane is at the 16-mile mark, and just along the road is the Well House Inn. The well from which the pub takes its name was mentioned in the Domesday Book. It's still there at the back of the pub but is now covered over.

The Well House Inn, Chipstead Lane, Coulsdon. Charringtons. 01737 832233. Open all day. Food G

At Hogden Bottom (17 miles) houses line one side of the lane and then the other before it ends at a roundabout on the A217 road near Lower Kingswood. Cross to the far side to reach the bridleway which leads onto Banstead Heath.

⑤ Banstead Heath to Margery Wood

The bridleway begins as a tarred drive, but this ends at a barrier on the edge of the heath.

The bridleway which heads off to the left beyond the barrier offers a direct route back to Mogador and Margery Wood, but recent diversions in its route have made it a rather uninteresting ride in parts. We have therefore opted for a longer but more scenic ride across the heath. Parts of it can be hard-going after wet weather.

From the barrier go straight ahead, taking the left fork when the track divides. The bridleway can be very muddy after rain, but there's a footpath parallel to it behind the hedge on your left, though if you do use it, please walk your bike. At the next path crossing, turn right, then immediately left, following the edge of the wood. Continue straight ahead when the track passes through a gap in the hedge which crosses your path. Soon after this the track veers to the left along the side of the garden of a house and into the woods.

At the next junction of paths (just over 18 miles), go straight ahead along the one signed 'Dorking Road 200 yards'. A short slope leads to the road.

Turn left along the road for about 100 yards, then turn left again (just after the bottom of the dip and opposite the sign for Walton House) onto another bridleway. It runs along the edge of Walton Heath golf course and marks the boundary of the one-time coal tax area, as the posts dotted about show.

Coal Tax posts, *made of cast iron, painted white, and bearing the City of London shield, mark the boundary of the area within which the City was once entitled to levy a tax on coal. The tax was originally charged on coal brought into the Port of London by sea but, as much of the traffic moved to the canals, railways and roads, the area within which the tax was levied was enlarged. The boundary marked by these posts was defined by an Act of Parliament of 1861. The tax was abolished in 1890.*

At the sign for the permissive horse ride go straight on, keeping to the right of the hedge and along the edge of the golf course. There's a pond a short distance further on and beyond that the track runs past a wooded area (19 miles). At a junction of tracks take the bridleway on the left signposted 'Mogador ¼ mile'. At the next fork, keep to the left for Mogador.

☞ *As an alternative, you can take the right-hand branch at this junction for the direct route back to Margery Wood. When you come to the drive of a house, go straight across, and then turn right at the road. Pass a house called Walton Gorse and then, immediately before one called*

Coal tax post

Thornymoor, turn left onto the bridleway signposted 'Margery Lane ½ mile'. When the bridleway crosses another road keep straight ahead along the fenced track until you eventually come to the car park (just over 20 miles).

You'll reach the road about 150 yards further on. To visit the Sportsman pub at Mogador, a lovely mid-18th century country pub situated on the very edge of Walton Heath at the end of a dead-end lane, turn to the left. Otherwise continue straight ahead along the road.

🖩 *The Sportsman, Mogador Road. Free house. 01737 246655. Food G*

There's a sharp dip in the road and then houses line the right-hand side (20 miles). At the next crossroads turn right, past the Mint Arms pub, named after the pepper-

Downland towers

mint which was once widely grown in this locality.

🏠 *The Mint Arms, Buckland Road. Friary Meux. 01737 248740. Open all day. Food*

Beyond the pub Buckland Road becomes a rough stony track, full of potholes. Follow it through to the end, which will bring you out by the entrance to the car park at Margery Wood, and the end of the ride (20½ miles).

Colley Hill: *Before you leave the car park at Margery Wood to head home, follow the footpath which leads off from its south-western corner. It crosses the motorway to reach Colley Hill, perhaps the most highly-rated of all the North Downs viewpoints.*

Ride H:
Outwood Bound

Outwood • Nutfield • Nutfield Marsh • Warwick Wold • Pendell • Brewer
Street • Bletchingley • Tilburstow Hill • South Park • Horne • Outwood

Distance: 15 miles
Landranger Maps: 187
Pathfinder Maps: 1207, 1227

This ride very nearly crosses Surrey from north to south, even if it is at one of
the county's narrowest points. Combine it with Ride I and you'll come within 2
miles of Greater London and half a mile of West Sussex. Remarkably, most of
the journey is on deserted country lanes and green byways. The ride runs
roughly parallel to the M23 motorway (and passes beneath it at two points),
but the contrast between the two routes could hardly be greater. This is truly
a ride in the spirit of William Cobbett.

The countryside through which the ride passes includes some of the most
charming and peaceful in Surrey, and the fact that much of it is inaccessible
to visitors in cars makes it all the more delightful. A 13th century deer park, a
farm stable converted into a chapel, the oldest windmill in working order in
the country, and a farmhouse which was once the gateway to a royal palace
are some of the more curious sights to be seen. The scenery varies from the
hilly ridges where sand and fuller's earth are quarried in massive pits near
Nutfield to the quiet fields of South Park.

The ride is mostly easy-going, although there are one or two steep ascents.
The off-road sections follow tracks which are either surfaced or in good
condition, and are unlikely to give problems, except after bad weather.

This ride was specially designed to link with Ride I as a way of travelling
across Surrey on 'hidden' lanes and tracks. Together they form a figure-of-
eight, centred on Outwood. You can decide whether to ride just one of the
loops or to tackle both rides in one go. One stretch of lane is included in both
rides, but less than a mile is involved.

Starting Points

You can start at Outwood, where there's
room to park on the edge of the common
opposite the windmill. However, it can
become busy at summer weekends. Not far
away from Outwood, on the road to
Bletchingley, there's a small National
Trust car park (free) at Bransland Wood.
There are two other parking places nearer
Bletchingley. One is a lay-by on the A25
east of the village (just beyond the Plough
Inn). The other (larger) one is at
Tilburstow Hill on Rabies Heath Road,
although this is just off the route. To join
the ride, turn left out of the car park and

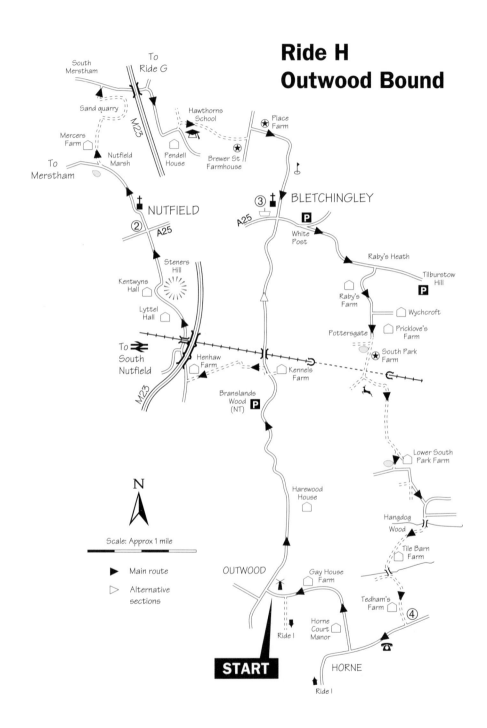

Ride H
Outwood Bound

ride down the hill until you come to the turning signposted 'Wychcroft & South Park'. Join the ride by turning left here. Remember, though, that you will end with a climb back to the top of Tilburstow Hill!

≽ The nearest station is at South Nutfield on the line from Redhill to Tonbridge. Go down the station approach until you come to Mid Street and then turn right. At the far end follow Kingcross Lane round to the left until you come to the junction with Coopers Hill Road by the M23 flyover. Turn left to join the route.

The Route in Brief

① From XR at Outwood follow SP for Bletchingley & Godstone. After Bransland Wood (CP) watch out for drive to Kennels Farm on R – TL here onto gravelled BW along inside of hedge. Follow BW to Henhaw Farm, through gate into farmyard and cross cattle-grid to reach road. TR onto road and keep SO to Nutfield XR.

② Cross A23 into Church Hill. Keep SO to green at Nutfield Marsh, then TR onto BW opposite Inn on the Pond sign. Follow BW past farm buildings into field. Keep to a line slightly R of straight ahead. At far side of field go through gate onto track serving sand quarry. Keep SO (may now have been diverted to R round edge of pit, rejoining old route on far side). Follow BW past school grounds to road. TR onto road and go under motorway. At next junc follow SP for Nutfield & Bletchingley.

TL into entrance of Pendell Court (Hawthorns School), then TR immediately after West Lodge. Follow BW to Brewer Street Farmhouse, then TL onto road. TR into Place Farm Road, SP Bletchingley & Godstone, and continue to main road at Bletchingley.

③ TL onto A25. After 200 yds or so TR into Rabies Heath Road. Climb hill then TR into lane SP Wychcroft & South Park. Follow

lane to gateway into South Park, then follow drive (BW) SO past pond and farm buildings. When track divides take L branch (concrete-surfaced). Pass small pond, after which track climbs gently. Pass through gate and follow track to L over brow of hill. When track divides take RF (dirt track) up gentle climb to wooden gate. Pass through and along gravelled drive past large pond to road. TL and follow tarred road to TJ. TR though private estate (road is BW). At sharp bend after 100 yds TR (SO) onto rough track (note blue BW arrow).

Follow BW through wood then past gateway of Tile Barn Farm. Continue on BW to and round farm buildings then along narrow stretch to gate with junc just beyond. TL up steep slope then SO past Tedhams Farm to road. TR onto road opposite pub.

√ Just after Ermine Cottage TR into Horne Court Hill, SP Outwood & Bletchingley. Climb hill and continue SO to Outwood (note lane becomes Gay House Lane at top of hill).

Outwood Mill

The Ride

Blechingley or Bletchingley? There's long been debate as to the way in which the village's name should be spelt. Many old documents show it without the 't', but nowadays the Post Office, the Ordnance Survey, and the local authorities have all adopted the form 'Bletchingley', especially on signposts. So, for consistency, shall we.

① Outwood to Nutfield

Outwood, *as its name implies, is situated on a sandstone outcrop that stands above the woodland of the Weald. It's famous for its extensive common, part of the 2000-acre Harewoods Estate, which was given to the National Trust in the 1950s. It's also famous for its windmill. Dating from 1665, it's the*

oldest post mill which is still in working order in England.

Until the 1960s there were two mills on the site – the post mill which survives today and a larger smock mill. The latter was built in 1860 as a rival to the post mill because of a dispute between the two brothers who were the millers. Post mills were designed to be turned around a central post, so that their sails could be brought into the wind. Smock mills – so-called because their shape resembled a farmworker's smock – were tower mills built of wood. The main structure was fixed, only the cap at the top being turned.

At Outwood the two mills became known as the Cat and the Kitten because of their relative sizes. Both became disused and eventually the smock mill collapsed, but the post mill has been restored and opens to the public Sunday and Bank Holiday afternoons, Easter–October. ☎ *01342 843458.*

▦ *The Bell, Outwood Lane, Outwood. Free house. 01342 842989. Open all day. Food G Rest*

From the crossroads near the windmill, set off in the direction signposted 'Bletchingley & Godstone'. The road bends as it leaves the common and heads downhill past the Bell Inn; this is a popular lunchtime venue for the local business community and can get very busy. It's claimed that King Charles II used to meet Nell Gwynne there.

Home Farm is a short distance along the lane. Once called Browne's farm (after an 18th century tenant) it later became the main farm of the Harewood Estate. Its oast house is a reminder of an industry which is not widely associated with this area today.

The lodge by the entrance to Harewood House itself is just along the lane, after which it passes a small area of woodland known as Brownshill Shaw (1 mile). From there the lane winds through fields and past Branslands Wood which, as a sign states, is owned by the National Trust. Just after a sharp left-hand bend there is a small car park on the left, beside which is a small pond (2 miles).

Immediately after the wood, as you approach the top of the rise, there are some lovely views to the left towards Reigate Hill, but keep an eye out on the right-hand side of the road for the drive to Kennels Farm.

☞ *From here the main route branches off to the left and reaches Bletchingley via Nutfield, Merstham and Pendell. If you wish to shorten the ride you can continue straight ahead along the road for about a mile and a half to reach Bletchingley.*

Turn in through the gate directly opposite the farm drive and follow the unsigned, gravelled bridleway which runs along the inside of the hedge. It heads towards a cottage for about 100 yards but then turns to the left along the side of its garden. After 400 yards the track zigzags right then left, before continuing towards Henhaw Farm, with views of the hills ahead. As you approach the farm, pass through a gate into the farmyard. After some cottages cross the cattle grid beside the large, red-brick farm building to reach the road (almost 3 miles).

Turn right onto the road, which climbs steeply for a short distance past Coopers Hill House. It appears that you are heading straight at the motorway, but when you reach the crest it is revealed that it crosses the valley on a surprisingly elegant viaduct, which the road dives to pass beneath. After the viaduct continue straight on past the turning to South Nutfield and under the railway bridge.

The road begins to climb quite steeply, passing Lyttel Hall, now the premises of BRF International, an anonymous name for what was formerly (and more

fascinatingly) the Brewing Research Foundation.

A brief respite in the climb onto the Greensand ridge is reached at Kentwyns Hall (about 4 miles); note the block for mounting horses (or cycles) in front of the house and the large pond in its garden. To the right of the road can be seen the prominent mound of Steners Hill.

There are more superb views from this stretch of road into the valleys and folds in the hills on the left, but these disappear all too soon as the road runs into a cutting in the sandstone. The climb finally ends shortly after this and the road heads down towards Nutfield crossroads.

Nutfield *sits astride the A25, which runs along the Greensand ridge at this point. The busy road dominates the centre of the village and, apart from refreshment, there is little reason to pause. The more scenic parts of the village are further out.*

Nutfield is most famous for the fuller's earth which is quarried at a site west of the village. Fulling is the process of removing grease from wool before it is spun, and fuller's earth has properties which aid this process. Extraction of the valuable material began in Roman times, if not earlier. As early as the reign of Edward II (1307–27) its export was forbidden in order to protect the country's wool and cloth industry. Today its main use is in oil refining and it's still much in demand yet hard to find, to the detriment of the scenery between Nutfield and Redhill.

The Crown, High Street. 01737 823240. Greene King. Sat 12–11, Sun 12–10.30. Food G. Coffee and soft drinks.

Queen's Head, High Street. 01737 822252. Friary Meux. Open all day. Food G

② Nutfield to Bletchingley

Cross the A25 into Church Hill. The lane descends steeply past the church, substantially restored in Victorian times, where the road becomes Nutfield Marsh Road. At the bottom of the hill are Peyton's Cottages, a delightful row of terraced 18th century houses, set back from the road beyond long front gardens. Apparently they were built as two separate terraces which were joined late in the last century. Just after the 5-mile point of the ride, the lane opens onto a wide, rough green. On the right is the tiny but enchanting Charman's Cottage. To the left is a pond and, overlooking it, the Inn on the Pond. Unless you are pausing for a drink, take the bridleway, on the right, opposite the pond.

The Inn on the Pond, Nutfield Marsh. Free house. 01737 643000. Open all day. Food G

The track passes a few cottages and farm outbuildings before disappearing into a field. Follow a line slightly to the right of straight ahead along what was, at the time of writing, a clear boundary between two old fields, though the hedge which once divided them has gone now. The ride is moderately bumpy but it shouldn't give too many problems.

At the far side of the field go through a gate onto a track serving a sand quarry. When this was written the bridleway continued straight ahead along a narrow strip between two separate quarries. The owners had proposed to divert the bridleway to the right around the edge of the pit, rejoining the original route on the far side, in order that the two quarries could be joined into one. This may have been carried out by now.

From the quarry the track passes some old school grounds before joining a road (6 miles). Turn right, and then in a short

Pendell House

while you'll pass through a cavernous arch under the M23. Beyond this is the junction with Warwick Wold Road, which leads to Chaldon and Caterham.

☞ *To link with Ride G turn left at this junction and continue for just over half a mile, crossing the M25, to the junction of Rockshaw Road, where the ride comes in from the left.*

Continue straight ahead in the direction of 'Nutfield & Bletchingley'. Merstham Road curves to run parallel with the M23, getting closer to it until, briefly, they are side by side. Then the road turns sharply away to the left and climbs away from the motorway. As it levels out you can see the back of the imposing Pendell House on the right.

Pendell *is little more than a cluster of three large houses. Pendell House was built in 1636 and it is said that Inigo Jones had at least a hand in its design. The elegant scalloped wall on the south side complements the house well but was not added until the mid-17th century. The arch in the wall was made high enough to allow a sedan chair to be carried under.*

Pendell Court, built in 1624, is now the Hawthorns School. There is a suspicion that the panelling in the hall may have been acquired from Bletchingley Place (see below). Pendell Manor House, further along the road, has no right to such a name – the manor house was Pendell Court. It was, in fact, an old tanhouse, which was extended and given a new front in the 18th century.

When the road begins to bend to the right around the grounds of Pendell House, turn left into the entrance of Pendell Court, which now houses the Hawthorns School. Two bridleways begin at this point; turn right immediately after the West Lodge for the correct one, which is called Water Lane. It's broad at first as it passes some old farm buildings, now converted into houses, but then it narrows as it

passes some school fields. It is an earth track but it appears to have a good foundation of stone. Nevertheless, there are some odd spots which could be muddy after wet weather.

As you approach the end of the track, you can see the back of the 15th century Brewer Street Farmhouse on the right. Unfortunately, this is not the best way to approach this historic building; the extensions at the rear are far less picturesque than the often-illustrated front facade. The track passes through the farmyard and out onto the road. The ride turns left here, but if you want to see the front of the house turn right, briefly.

Pass the stable block, now converted into small commercial units, and then turn right into Place Farm Road, signposted 'Bletchingley & Godstone'. Place Farm is about 100 yards along the road on the left. Be sure to pause at the end of the drive leading to it.

Place Farm *is all that remains of Bletchingley Place, built in about 1517 by the Duke of Buckingham, who then owned the manor. For nearly ten years after 1540 it was the home of Anne of Cleves, the divorced fourth wife of Henry VIII. Their marriage was intended to foster a foreign alliance, but when she arrived in England Henry was astounded by her extreme plainness, a detail which had been kept from him. The marriage lasted only six months.*

The farmhouse was adapted from the old gatehouse, and the arch of the former gateway can still be seen, although it's now blocked and has an 18th century door set into it. The remains of the foundations of the rest of the building apparently still exist in the field behind the house.

Just beyond Place Farm there's a large pond on the right (8 miles) and shortly afterwards the road bends to the right and becomes Church Lane. Bletchingley

Church, with its solid Norman tower, is visible ahead. Look through the hedge on the left and you are looking along the fields of the Vale of Holmesdale in the direction of Godstone. Framed by the downs to the north and the Greensand hills to the south, the fertile soil of this valley is gault clay, enriched by sand and chalk washed down from the hills. There is a steady climb past Bletchingley Golf Club towards the village.

Pass the church, and continue towards the main road. Immediately beyond the churchyard is Church House. The original main road through the village was the narrow path which is now known as Church Walk. It continued through the site of Church House and along the footpath on the left, joining the present road near the Plough pub.

Bletchingley *was created as a town late in the 12th or early 13th century by the de Clare*

family, the Norman overlords who controlled much of east Surrey and west Kent. The new town was probably developed at the expense of the existing nearby Saxon settlement of Chevington (or Civentone), which was further to the east, towards Godstone.

Two features remain from the town's earliest days. One is the wide space at its eastern end, which was the site of the market place. The second, at the other end, is the mound which was the base of the castle. It was first mentioned as being one of four castles in Surrey, and may even have been built soon after the Conquest in 1066.

In 1264 it played a part in the rebellion of Simon de Montford when Gilbert de Clare fought against the King, Henry III. Although the King lost that clash and was taken prisoner, Bletchingley castle was captured by the royalist army. De Clare made amends the following year by supporting the King when he was restored to the throne after the battle of Evesham, but it appears the castle's days were numbered. Recent excavations have shown it only ever had timber defences, not stone, and the building that the mound supported was more a house than keep. It was probably demolished in 1264.

Compared with other 'castle towns' such as Reigate, Guildford and Tonbridge, the development of Bletchingley into a major centre appears to have halted with the destruction of the castle, although it did later become a borough. Indeed, it became infamous as one of the 'rotten boroughs' which sent members to Parliament, despite having a tiny number of voters. Bletchingley had two MPs but only some 40 or 50 voters. The borough was abolished by the Reform Act of 1832. Lord Palmerston was one of its last members.

The Prince Albert, Old Market Place. Friary Meux. 01883 743257. Food

The White Hart, Old Market Place. Free House. 01883 743231. Open all day (Sun 12–10.30) Food G C Acc

The Plough Inn, Godstone Road. Millers Kitchen. 01883 743711. Open all day Food (all day)

Longhursts, newsagents, Old Market Place.

③ Bletchingley to Horne

At the end of Church Lane turn left onto Godstone Road. Although this is the busy A25 we shall be using it for only a couple of hundred yards. If you prefer, you can walk your bike along the pavement.

The road dips just beyond the Plough Inn (9 miles) and you may think there should be a bridge across a stream at the bottom. At one time there was, but the stream, the Funk Brook, was piped in 1870.

A re-alignment of the road has left a lay-by which may be useful for parking; you can also ride through it to avoid the main road traffic. At the end of the lay-by turn

Bletchingley

South Park

Bletchingley's first deer park, North Park, was probably established soon after the Norman Conquest, when the manor was given to Earl Richard of Tonbridge, a cousin of William the Conqueror and head of the de Clare family. The South Park seems to date from 1233, when Roger de Clare, a kinsman of the then Earl, was given ten hinds and two stags from the North Park to stock one of his own. The new park covered 1600 acres, stretching a mile from the Outwood–Bletchingley road in the west to the parish boundary in the east, and about two miles from north to south.

Both parks were broken up in about 1650 as a result of the Civil War, when the royalist Earl of Peterborough, the lord of the manor, had to sell the land to pay his debts. The North Park was divided into three smaller farms, Place Farm, which you passed earlier on the ride, being one of them. South Park, being larger, was split into six farms, including South Park Farm and Lower South Park. Near one of the others, Lodge Farm, is a curious rectangular earthwork, the purpose of which is far from certain. It's been suggested that it could be the site of a short-lived castle or of a chapel (indeed, it's called Chapel Plat), but it was most likely an enclosure for keeping deer, perhaps while they were breeding.

Among the buildings at South Park Farm is St Mark's Chapel. It was converted in 1909 from a 17th century stable by Mr Uvedale Lambert, the owner of the farm (and lord of the manor), to give thanks for the birth of his son, also named Uvedale. In 1912 the roof caught fire – scorch marks caused by burning debris can still be seen on the floor.

In July 1944 a V1 bomb landed on the farm, killing Mrs Diana Lambert and destroying part of the house and the chapel. It seems particularly tragic that, in the midst of so much open countryside, an unguided, pilotless bomb should fall to earth here. The chapel was again rebuilt, being re-opened in 1949. The west door came from Hever Castle in Kent. The original part of the farmhouse, just beyond the chapel, was destroyed by the V1. Of it only the wall containing the white garden gate survives. The west front of the house was built after the war, but in 18th century style.

A door in one of the farm buildings bears a sign "St Mark's Foundation – Information". You are welcome to enter this room, which contains displays about the history of the park and the farm, and the natural history of the area. There are also local history books and walk notes for sale. There's even a kettle with which you can brew yourself a drink, and some chairs to rest on! (The Foundation is a religious and educational charity which was established to provide a centre for reflection and prayer in a country setting.)

right into Rabies Heath Road. This junction was once known as Catherine's Cross but is now called White Post. It's signposted 'Tilburstow Hill' and there are also signs for the Surrey Cycleway.

At first you may think you have turned into a suburban housing estate – a post-war estate of council-built houses has been enlarged by the redevelopment of an old hospital site – but this is soon left behind. The road begins to climb, giving good views towards the Downs on the left. It passes Brick Kiln Cottage – a complete contrast to the previous houses – and then it climbs much more steeply.

As you climb watch for the entrance to Raby's Heath House. (The heath is named after John Rabie, who owned land here in the 16th century.) Immediately beyond it, take the turning on the right (known as Snatts Hill), signposted 'Wychcroft &

South Park', ignoring the no-through-road sign (10 miles).

The lane descends steeply. Magnificent views over the Weald open up before you, and a bicycle seat is the perfect vantage point from which to see over the hedges. Car-borne tourists, assuming they ever come this way, are deprived of all this. The timber-framed cottage tucked away at the foot of the hill is Raby's Farm, around which the lane curves sharply. Keep going past the side-turning to Wychcroft, a Victorian mansion now used as a training centre for the Diocese of Southwark.

Just after Prickloves Farm, the lane passes through a gateway, beyond which unauthorised vehicles are prohibited. This is Pottersgate, once the north entrance of South Park. Keep going straight on when you come to a triangular junction just beyond a couple of cottages, then make

South Park Farm

Through the fields of South Park

your way between neat grass verges and past a pond, towards the farm buildings.

South Park Farm *has a fascinating history (see panel) and today it's such a remote and enchanting place, you cannot believe you are less than 25 miles from the centre of London! Fortunately, you have to know it's there to find it, and then you can only reach it on foot, horse or bike. Few do, so its peace and quiet are unruffled. Long may it stay that way.*

The lane continues along the side of the garden wall, and with outbuildings on the right, but there's another surprise in store in this delightful place. In the middle of the garden wall is a door which is also marked with a St Marks' sign. The gardens within are privately owned, but they are open most of the time for visitors to enjoy, quietly and unobtrusively. They are certainly worth seeing.

Continue along the lane past the old dairy and out into open countryside beyond

(11 miles). Beneath the fields runs the Bletchingley railway tunnel, built in 1841, and the thicket on the left conceals one of its ventilation shafts. You may hear trains approaching in the distance, only for the sound to disappear suddenly.

A little further on, when the track divides (the right-hand branch passes through a gate), follow the concrete track round to the left. (For most of the next mile or so it is either concreted or has a good stone formation.) After a short distance the track bends to the left and then the right, passing a small pond which is probably a relic of iron smelting in the 18th century. From the bend there is a gentle climb through the fields. Watch out for the tree on the left with a woodpecker's nest hole.

Approaching the top of the hill the track comes to a gate, after which it veers to the left. This is a very tranquil spot, and an ideal place from which to watch birds and wildlife. Beyond the brow of the hill another concrete section of track begins, but when it divides a short way further on (about 12 miles), take the right-hand branch – a dirt track. There's another gentle climb to a wooden gate. Go through the small gate on the right and continue straight ahead along the gravelled drive past the outstanding buildings of Lower South Park Farm. There's a large pond on the right.

Lower South Park Farm, *like the other farms in the old park, was built in the mid-17th century when the park was divided up. The old barn was also built at this time, but was converted late in the 19th century into a hall for parties.*

When you come out on the lane at the end of the drive, turn left and follow it past some rather incongruous modern houses and bungalows. Beyond these the lane curves to the right and climbs gently. At the top of the hill, stay on the tarred road as it bends to the left, ignoring the rough track going straight on.

After a short wooded stretch the lane comes to a junction. Turn right along a road through a private estate of houses, set in sizeable grounds. After a hundred yards or so, the road bends sharply to the left – leave the road here and continue straight ahead onto a rough track marked by a blue bridleway waymark arrow. It crosses a small stream and heads into Hangdog Wood (13 miles).

At the far end of the wood the track passes through a brick-pillared gateway into the fields of Tile Barn Farm. When you get to the farmhouse it curves to the right to avoid the front of the house. Beyond the farm there is a short narrow stretch which

Lower South Park

can be overgrown. It leads to a gate, with a junction immediately beyond. This is Tedham Gate, which once marked the southern limit of South Park.

Turn left, and climb a short but steep slope, after which the track becomes more open and runs downhill. The white-painted farmhouse is now called Tedhams Farm. According to Uvedale Lambert's history of Bletchingley, it was once called Charity Farm because it was where the parish charity put the poor to work. Continue down the track to the road, opposite the Jolly Farmer pub (14 miles).

The pub was once a farm cottage until it was converted in 1788, as the date on the front wall shows, or was it 1878? It once had racks over the fireplaces on which gamekeepers could hang their guns. Today it offers a convenient opportunity for refreshment before a strenuous bout of hill-climbing.

The Jolly Farmer. Free house. 01342 842867. Food G

√ Horne to Outwood

Turn right out of the bridleway opposite the Jolly Farmer (left if you're coming out of the pub). There's a card-operated phone box just along the road, by the small hamlet of Whitewood. The road climbs gently towards Horne village, but instead of continuing into the village, turn right just after Ermine Cottages into Horne Court Hill, signposted 'Outwood & Bletchingley'.

The road soon begins to climb, but after Horne Court Manor Farm – once described as looking like a workhouse – it becomes steep for the next few hundred yards as it climbs the hill on which Outwood is situated. The gradient eases as you pass Horne Court Cottage (where the lane becomes Gay House Lane, once the southern boundary of South Park) and

finally levels out at Gay House, another of the 17th century farms created out of the park (just over 15 miles). You can see the mill at Outwood ahead, and by looking to the left you can see how prominent a hill this is, and why it proved an ideal site for a windmill.

☞ *At this point you must decide whether to continue on Ride I or end here. To end, continue along the lane until you come to the windmill and the start point (15½ miles). To continue with Ride I, turn left at the white bungalow called Knowl Green, shortly before you get to the windmill.*

Ride I:
The Miller's Trail

Outwood • Wilmot's Farm • Bysshe Court • Chithurst • West Park • East Park • Horne Park • Horne • Horne Court • Outwood

Distance:	9 miles
Landranger Maps:	187
Pathfinder Maps:	1227

Starting from the windmill at Outwood, this ride takes in some of the loneliest imaginable countryside in Surrey. The outward leg of the journey is along nearly four miles of deserted off-road tracks, which take you close to the Sussex border. The return is along lanes which are almost as remote. Apart from the occasional planes flying in to Gatwick Airport, you could wonder if you were not a hundred miles or more from London.

The ride is very gentle, apart from the final climb past Horne Court Manor. The off-road tracks are in good condition, and are unlikely to cause any difficulties. The ride does, though, include a mile along the busy B2028 road, but we have suggested an alternative return route to avoid this if you prefer.

The ride can be enjoyed on its own or it can be linked with Ride H to create a 24-mile loop across from the north to the south of the county.

Starting Points

There is room to park on the edge of the common at Outwood opposite the windmill, but space can be scarce at weekends. Not far from Outwood, on the road to Bletchingley, there's a small, free National Trust car park at Bransland Wood. If you are combining this ride with Ride H, see the description of that ride for additional parking places.

≋ The remoteness of this ride means there are no railway stations within a short distance of the route. The nearest is three miles away at Lingfield, served by Connex South Central services on the London Victoria–East Grinstead line. To join the ride take the B2028 west from Lingfield, and take the second turning on the right after the A22 at Newchapel.

Ride I
The Miller's Trail

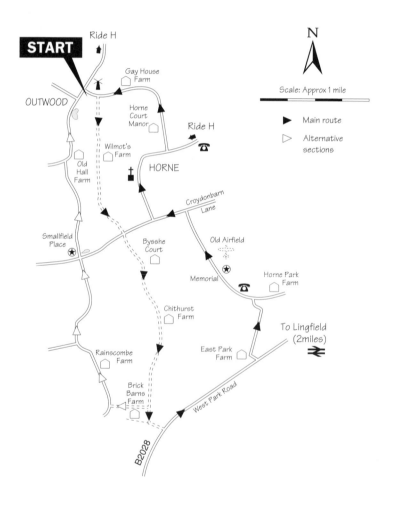

START

Ride H

OUTWOOD

Gay House Farm

Horne Court Manor

Ride H

Wilmot's Farm

Old Hall Farm

HORNE

Croydonbarn Lane

Smallfield Place

Bysshe Court

Old Airfield

Memorial

Horne Park Farm

Chithurst Farm

To Lingfield
(2miles)

Rainscombe Farm

East Park Farm

Brick Barns Farm

West Park Road

B2028

N

Scale: Approx 1 mile

▶ Main route

▷ Alternative sections

The Route in Brief

① From Outwood XR start along Gay House Lane, SP Horne. After a very short distance TR onto BY immediately after white bungalow 'Knowl Green'. Keep SO along BY. At Wilmot's Farm it becomes the tarred Wilmot's Lane. Continue to junc with road by Whitegates Boarding Kennels. TL then TR into Chithurst Lane. Continue past Bysshe Court Farm, Holmleigh Farm, and Chithurst Farm to junc in track near Brick Barns.

② As tarred track bends away to R, continue SO between posts onto dirt track. Follow it round bend to L past Downswood Cottage to road (B2028), then TL. Continue on road to first turning (about 1 mile) then TL. At next junc TL. Continue through old airfield. At following TJ TL, SP Horne & Smallfield, then TR into Church Lane, SP Horne, Blindley Heath & Godstone. Go through village then take next on L, Horne Court Hill, SP Outwood & Bletchingley. Continue up hill to Outwood.

Surrey country lane

The Ride

① Outwood to Brick Barns

From the windmill at Outwood Common, take Gay House Lane in the direction signposted 'Horne' for a short distance, before turning right onto a byway immediately beyond a white-painted bungalow called Knowl Green.

The first part of the byway, beside the house, is gravelled; beyond a sign stating 'Unsuitable for Motors' the track is surfaced with roadworks scrapings and is in good condition. There's a deep ditch on one side to provide the drainage which is so badly needed on the Weald Clay. A gentle downhill run makes for pleasant riding.

At Wilmot's Farm, with its couple of ponds, the track becomes a tarred lane. Because it's a dead-end there's virtually no traffic and it makes for a superb ride. Across the field to the left you can see Horne church and after the 1-mile point there are a few scattered cottages and houses along the lane – Paradise Cottage is particularly well-named – but they do not intrude into the rural scene.

At the end of Wilmot's Lane, by the Whitegates Boarding Kennels, turn left then immediately right into Chithurst Lane, ignoring the 'no through road' sign. Beware of fast-moving traffic as you cross the junction.

Bysshe Court Farm takes its name from the Bysshe family who lived at nearby Smallfield Place during the tumultuous years of the 17th century. The poet Percy Bysshe Shelley was a distant, but later, relation. Like many houses and farms hereabouts, Bysshe Court Farm is moated (you cannot see it from the lane), but this was done less for defence than for drainage and status. The lack of defensive purpose is indicated by the fact that most of the important storage buildings were left outside the moat.

There's a slight climb past Holmleigh Farm (2 miles) onto a level plateau, from which there are views back towards the North Downs. Woodland to the right adds variety to the open fields. The only jarring note in this otherwise tranquil scene is that the flightpath of Gatwick Airport passes directly overhead! Chithurst Farm, which dates from about 1700 (B&B offered) is a short way ahead, after which there's a run of about three-quarters of a mile through open country. At Brick Barns Farm (3 miles) the lane swings to the right and the bridleway continues straight ahead onto a dirt track, passing between two posts.

② Brick Barns to Outwood

☞ *The next part of the ride involves a mile ride along the B2028 road, which can be busy and fast-moving at times. It's worth putting up with this, though, for the ride through Horne. However, if you'd prefer to avoid the traffic, follow the alternative route on page 132.*

About 250 yards after Brick Barns, the track bends to the left past Downswood Cottage, and in another 250 yards it comes out onto the main B2028 road at West Park. Turn left onto the road, taking great care because of the traffic. There's not a great deal to see along this stretch, and you really need to keep your attention on the road.

Turn off at the next turning on the left, after a little more than a mile (just over 4½ miles). The turning, called East Park Lane, is not signed but is heralded by a junction sign. After the busy road it's wonderful to be back on a quiet country lane. The lane bends to the right at the

Memorial at RAF Horne

entrance of East Park Farm and then ambles down past Little Brook Farm.

At the next junction (5 miles) the ride continues to the left, but it's worth a short diversion to the right as far as Horne Park Farm. This mid-19th century farmhouse, far from being picturesque in the traditional sense, has a severe symmetry, coupled with an almost-French look which gives it a strange attractiveness, particularly in such a remote spot.

Turn left out of East Park Lane into Bones Lane. There's a small hamlet here, with a village hall and a timberyard; there's also a phone box. Glen Farm, on the right, is startlingly modern, but in the traditional style. Immediately beyond it the road curves to the right. Watch out on the right-hand side of the road, just at the start of a long length of post and rail fencing, for a small stone monument.

RAF Horne: *As the plaque describes, the fields on either side of the lane here were the site of RAF Horne, an advanced landing ground built to support the D-Day landings in 1944. Three squadrons of Spitfires, from India. Poland and Canada, were based here for a few weeks. The two (grass) runways crossed the road just north of the monument. Look carefully and the fields still show some signs of their short wartime occupation, and the lack of hedges and roadside ditches provides further lasting evidence.*

Continue along the lane, past a golf driving range, to the junction at its end (just over 6 miles).

Turn left in the direction of 'Horne & Smallfield', then, after about a quarter of a mile, turn right into Church Road, which is signposted 'Horne, Blindley Heath & Godstone'. Horne village is a few hundred yards further on.

East Park • Horne Park • Horne Airfield 131

Horne is a tiny settlement today, consisting of little more than a church, a village school, now closed and used as the Yew Tree Nursery, and a few houses. The school was opened only in 1910 – formal education obviously came late to this remote spot. The nursery takes its name from the several yews which grow in the churchyard, some of which have reached a good height. The village is small, but the parish (which was separated from Bletchingley only in 1705) is quite large with several scattered settlements. The village was not always so quiet. In 1332 it had a population of around 200, which was quite substantial.

Continue along the lane from the village to the junction of Horne Court Hill (just over 7 miles), and then turn left in the direction of Outwood and Bletchingley. (This stretch of road is also covered in Ride H.)

The road soon begins to climb the hill towards Outwood – and it soon becomes clear why that spot was chosen to site a windmill. The steepest stretch is between Horne Court Manor Farm and Horne Court Cottage, before eventually levelling out at Gay House (about 8 miles). When you get to the top of the hill pause for a moment to look back and enjoy the tremendous view. It's now only a short run back to the common and the end of the ride (8½ miles).

Alternative section of route

② Brick Barns to Outwood

☞ *This alternative avoids the ride along the busy B2028, but it's also an attractive ride in its own right.*

The surfaced lane curving off to the right at Brick Barns is a private lane which is only a public right of way as a footpath. Strictly speaking, you should walk your bike along this stretch, but there'll probably not be any complaints if you ride discreetly.

At the end of the lane, turn right into Dowlands Lane and follow it northwards past Rainscombe Farm and Dowlands Farm. Continue straight ahead at the junction with Cross Lane (just over 4 miles). From there the lane winds about through the countryside until it comes to a crossroads (just under 5 miles).

Cross over into Cogman's Lane, taking care because of the traffic. On the right beyond the junction is Long Pond, and directly opposite, behind high walls which the height of a cycle makes it possible to see over, is Smallfield Place, previously mentioned as the home of the Bysshes. It was built about 1600.

Continue along the lane, climbing gently, to the junction with Scotts Hill at its far end (6 miles). Turn right, past Old Hall Farm, and climb the steep hill towards Outwood. The large Marl Pond on the right marks the top of the climb and heralds the end of the ride, which is just ahead at the crossroads by the windmill (6¾ miles).

Ride J:
East (and West) of Eden

Lingfield • Dormans • Dry Hill • Starborough • Haxted • Dwelly • Merle Common • Broadham Green • Hurst Green • Old Oxted • Barrow Green • Tandridge • Crowhurst • Lingfield Common • Lingfield

Distance:	18 or 24 miles
Landranger Maps:	187
Pathfinder Maps:	1207, 1227, 1228

Unlike the major Surrey rivers, the Wey and the Mole, which make their way through gaps in the North Downs to join the Thames, East Surrey's less well-known Eden heads into Kent to join the Medway. With its numerous small tributaries, most of them little more than streams and ditches, it drains a wide area of fairly flat countryside south of Oxted.

The route stays close to the Eden itself and its main tributaries, the Eden Brook and the Gibbs Brook, passing through remote, low-lying fields, although the northern and southern extremities of the ride are hilly. The countryside is pleasant and there's plenty of interest to see. A couple of charming small towns, a handful of unspoiled villages and hamlets, superb old buildings, and some historic sites along the way, make this a ride worth taking time over.

Starting Points

By far the easiest place to leave a car is in Lingfield, which can be reached off the main A22 Godstone–East Grinstead road by either the B2028 or B2029. There's a large free car park in Gunpit Road, just off Plaistow Street, right in the town centre, but it can get busy with shoppers on Saturdays.

In contrast, Old Oxted is very short of car parking space, and is best avoided, but there are several car parks in Oxted itself, not too far from the route. On the more rural part of the ride, there's a car park near St Silvan's Church, close to Merle

Common (grid reference TQ 410487), but other than this, there are only occasional lay-bys and roadside verges.

≥ The route passes close to stations at Oxted, Hurst Green, Dormans, and Lingfield. All are served by regular Connex South Central trains on the London–East Croydon–East Grinstead line. Edenbridge Town is on the same company's Oxted–Uckfield branch line but is about 2½ miles from the ride. Edenbridge is on the Tonbridge–Redhill line run by Connex South Eastern and is about 2 miles off the route.

Ride J
East (and West) of Eden

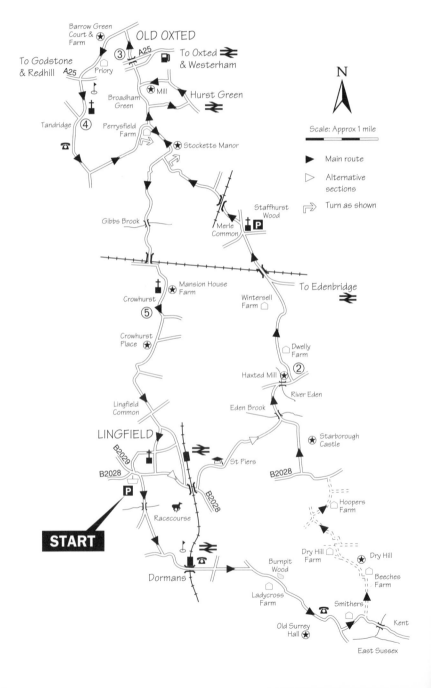

Barrow Green
Court & ⭐
Farm

OLD OXTED

③ A25

To Oxted ⇌
& Westerham

To Godstone
& Redhill A25

Priory

⭐ Mill

Hurst Green ⇌

Broadham
Green

Tandridge ④

Perrysfield
Farm

Stocketts Manor

☎

N

Scale: Approx 1 mile

▶ Main route

▷ Alternative
sections

⇨ Turn as shown

Gibbs Brook

Staffhurst
Wood

☩ P

Merle
Common

Mansion House
Farm

To Edenbridge ⇌

Crowhurst

⭐

Wintersell
Farm

⑤

Crowhurst
Place ⭐

Dwelly
Farm

Haxted Mill ⭐

②

River Eden

Lingfield
Common

Eden Brook

Starborough
Castle ⭐

LINGFIELD

B2029

⇌

St Piers

B2028

B2028

P

B2028

Hoopers
Farm

Racecourse

START

Dry Hill ☐   Dry Hill ⭐

Burnpit
Wood

Beeches
Farm

Dormans

☎

Ladycross
Farm

Smithers ☎

Kent

Old Surrey
Hall ⭐

East Sussex

The Route in Brief

① From CP TR out of Gunpit Road, then R again at mini-roundabout into East Grinstead Road, SP Felcourt & East Grinstead. At bottom of hill (Jacks Bridge) TL into Blackberry Lane, SP Dormansland. At next TJ TL. Pass Dormans Stn. Keep SO at next XR, SP Cowden & Tunbridge Wells. TR at following TJ.

Soon after sharp right bend (phonebox on corner), TL into narrow unsigned lane. At bottom of hill TL at triangular junc onto BW, SP Woodlands Farm & Beeches Farm. At first set of farm buildings keep L, following sign for Beeches Farm. At Beeches Farm follow BW signs to L then R round farm. Continue through wood then up side of field (rough), then follow track as it bears L across field towards gap in hedge. Keep SO along edge of field beyond, through Dry Hill Fort.

At corner of reservoir follow track to L through banks of fort, then keep SO towards Dry Hill Farm, but when track divides keep to R. At junc by houses TR. Pass cottages then TL onto BW immediately before trees. Follow BW along series of zigzags then through wood.

Pass through two successive tubular metal gates then TR towards farm. Keep to main farm track, passing though farmyard out out of farm gate. Pass house, following track to L, then through another gate. Keep SO to junc with B2028 and TL. After quarter of a mile TR into lane, SP Haxted. Continue to TJ at far end then TR, SP Haxted.

② Continue east from Haxted Mill up steep hill then TL before top into Dwelly Lane, SP Oxted & Limpsfield. Continue for about 2½ miles to TJ (by sign for Royal Oak pub) then TR. After 100 yds FL into lane SP Hurst Green & Merle Common. Under railway then keep SO, SP Broadham Green & Tandridge.

At TJ at far end TR, SP Broadham Green, Oxted & Tandridge. Another TJ follows – TR, SP Hurst Green & Oxted. At Broadham Green TR into Tanhouse Road, SP Hurst Green & Limpsfield, past Haycutter pub, then at far end TL into Woodhouse Lane, for Oxted. Continue for about half a mile then TL into narrow Spring Lane, (not signed). Pass Oxted Mill and continue up steep hill to TJ. TR into Beadles Lane to reach Old Oxted.

③ Keep SO at Old Oxted XR into Sandy Lane. At TJ at far end TL into Barrow Green Road. Continue to XR at A25, then cross over and keep SO to Tandridge church.

√ From church continue over top of rise and past Barley Mow pub. At TJ beyond village TL into Southlands Lane. Continue for 1 mile then take next on R, SP Crowhurst & Edenbridge. (You have covered next stretch in opposite direction.) At junc with Popes Lane keep SO, SP Crowhurst & Lingfield. After 1½ miles cross railway and TL. Pass through Crowhurst.

⑤ From village keep SO past two turnings on L, and past Crowhurst Place gatehouse. Continue to junc at Lingfield Common. TR then immediately L, SP Dormansland & Lingfield. At outskirts of Lingfield FR into Saxbys Lane, SP Lingfield. At Vicarage Road XR continue SO into Church Road. At next XR TR. At mini-roundabout TR into Plaistow Street then TL into Gunpit Road.

The Ride

① Lingfield to Haxted Mill

☞ *This part of the ride involves a lengthy off-road stretch through Dry Hill Fort. An alternative road route is given on page 146.*

From the car park, turn right out of Gunpit Road, and then, at the mini-roundabout, turn right into East Grinstead Road, signposted 'Felcourt & East Grinstead'. The road heads out of the town, winding gently downhill to Jacks Bridge, where it crosses the Eden Brook. Immediately beyond, after the bridge, bear left into Blackberry Lane, following the signs for 'Dormansland'.

The lane runs along the side of Lingfield racecourse, which can be glimpsed through the hedge on the left, and then

Lingfield Cage

starts to climb out of the valley, gently at first, but then steeper. The top of the climb is reached at Folly Down Farm (1 mile), about 300 yards after which is a T-junction, opposite the beautifully-landscaped gardens of a private house. Turn left, and pass, on your left, one of Surrey's innumerable golf courses.

Climbing once more, the road passes the entrance to Dormans Park and, just beyond this, a corrugated iron fence on the left hides the end of the racecourse's 'straight mile'. The hill steepens after the entrance to the College of St Barnabas, climbing to the bridge over the railway at Dormans Station, where there's a tele-phone box.

Shortly after the station the road passes Starborough Cottages, built in 1822, before it comes to a crossroads (2 miles). Go straight on, following the signs for 'Cowden & Tunbridge Wells', but cautiously, because the other road is busy. The climb continues for a few hundred yards beyond the crossroads, but then the road descends to a T-junction. Turn right here.

The next stretch of road is easy, mostly level riding. Look out on the left-hand side, opposite Ladycross Farm, for the lake in Burnpit Wood. Shortly after this, the road passes the track leading to Dry Hill Farm (almost 3 miles). The ride passes through this farm, but gets there by a more round-about, but interesting, route.

Another climb brings you past the entrance of Old Surrey Hall, a moated farmhouse of around 1450, which was substantially rebuilt and extended by George Crawley in 1922, although in skilful imitation of the earlier style.

There are some marvellous views as the road first levels out and then runs down-hill. A row of cottages signals a sharp bend to the right, with a phone box on the corner. About 300 yards further down the road, turn left into a narrow, unsigned lane (4 miles), which leads down the hill to a charming cottage called Smithers. This is almost the end of Surrey. Indeed, three counties come together not very far from this spot – Surrey, Kent, and East Sussex. A small bridge over a stream a short distance along the road marks the border with Kent, but the ride turns off to the left just before that, at a triangular junction, onto the bridleway signposted to Woodlands Farm and Beeches Farm.

The bridleway is surfaced, but climbs steeply from the road. When you come to the first set of farm buildings, keep to the left, following the sign to Beeches Farm. When you reach that farm (5 miles), follow the bridleway signs to the left and then, immediately afterwards, to the right, skirting around the farm itself. The track becomes more informal now. Follow it straight on through a wooded area and then up a slope along the right-hand edge of a field, where it becomes extremely rough. As you near the top of the slope, follow the track as it curves to the left across the field, heading for a gap in the hedge.

As you pass through the gap you'll see that the hedge is set on a raised bank. From there the track continues along the edge of another field, which occupies part of the site of Dry Hill Fort. There are some tremendous views from this vantage point, but it can be very exposed in inclement weather.

Dry Hill Fort *is an Iron Age hill-fort situated on one of the most prominent heights in the south-east corner of Surrey. It's surrounded by a system of banks and ditches, up to three in number, parts of which are still clearly visible. There are a number of these sites throughout Surrey, but we still have little understanding of their purpose and use. They may not have been for purely defensive purposes, but may*

have served as trading centres, tribal head-quarters, or religious sites. Two excavations of Dry Hill found little sign of occupation as a settlement, but the presence of slag suggests it was an iron-working site.

Part of the hilltop is used by an underground reservoir, surrounded by an iron fence. When you reach the corner of the reservoir, follow the track round to the left and out through the banks of the fort, which can be seen quite clearly on the left.

The track continues downhill towards Dry Hill Farm, and there are marvellous views northwards towards the Downs. As you head towards the farm, keep to the right to stay on the main track; don't be tempted to follow the edge of the field as it heads towards the farm buildings.

The track leads to a junction by some houses, where you turn right. Go past some cottages and take the waymarked bridleway on the left immediately before the trees. The bridleway is quite narrow and, although there are one or two sticky patches, it's not in too bad condition.

The first part of the bridleway zigzags its way, in a most intriguing fashion, through a series of bends around the edge of a wood. When it does, at last, enter the wood (6 miles), it becomes quite rough, and you may need to dismount. Watch for a step by some old wooden gates (which are normally left open). The track soon emerges from the trees and, from the crest just ahead, there are some good views to the north.

When you come to a tubular metal farmgate, go through it and continue to a second, similar gate. Go through it as well, then turn to the right, heading towards the buildings of Hoopers Farm. Keep to the main farm track, ignoring the bridleway heading to the left through an avenue of trees. Go through the farm and out of the farmgate (watch for the muddy spot). Pass a house, following the track to the left, and then go through another gate. The next stretch is easy riding, past a side turning (to New Barns Farm) and on to a junction with the B2028 Lingfield–Edenbridge road. Turn left, passing the Old Forge (7 miles).

After a quarter of a mile, turn right into the lane signposted 'Haxted'; Starborough Nurseries is a short distance along the way. The next stretch of countryside is flat, as the road threads its way across the meadows of the Eden valley. To the right, about 400 yards away, is Starborough Castle.

Starborough Castle *was the home of the Cobham family, whose memorials fill Lingfield church. The castle was built by the first Lord Cobham in 1342. One of the greatest soldiers of the time, he fought at the battle of Crécy and became wealthy from ransoms paid for the prisoners he took. The second Lord Cobham*

was one of the commissioners who ruled while Richard II was a minor, and was subsequently exiled by him. He became a supporter of Henry Bolingbroke, who was crowned Henry IV after overthrowing Richard.

The third Lord Cobham fought at Agincourt, and was warden of the Duke of Orleans who was taken prisoner at Agincourt and afterwards held at Starborough. This was the Lord Cobham who was responsible for rebuilding Lingfield church. He died in 1446 and, incredibly, within 25 years the family, which had played such an important part in the turbulent affairs of the previous two centuries, had died out.

The castle was slightly earlier than, but apparently rather similar in construction to, that at Bodiam in East Sussex, with four towers and a gate. Unlike Bodiam, though, Starborough (or Sterborough as it was once called) has not survived. It was garrisoned for Parliament in the Civil War in 1648, but then dismantled to prevent it being taken by the

Haxted Mill

Royalists. Only the moat and a few foundations remain. The battlemented summerhouse on the site was not built until 1754, and the present house around 1880.

Shortly after the entrance to Starborough Farm, the road bends sharply to the left (8 miles) and, a few hundred yards after that, it passes a junction on the left, and crosses a recently-rebuilt bridge over the Eden Brook.

☞ *The alternative route from Lingfield via St Piers rejoins here.*

The lane continues for another half-mile to a T-junction. Turn right, in the direction of Haxted. Note the raised wooden footway, provided for those occasions when the low-lying road is flooded. The river which causes these problems is a couple of hundred yards along the road at Haxted Mill.

Haxted Mill *is a fully-restored watermill on the River Eden. The present building was constructed late in the 18th century, although parts are probably older, as the site was occupied long before that. Its weather-boarded construction is more typical of Kent than of Surrey. The mill was last used commercially in 1945, and was subsequently restored to working order as a museum. Open Easter–end October (including Bank Hols); closed Mon. Adults £1, children 75p.*

② Haxted Mill to Old Oxted

From the mill continue eastwards up a steep hill but, before you get to the top, turn left into Dwelly Lane, which is signposted 'Oxted & Limpsfield'. Beyond Haxted Kennels (9 miles) is a stretch of very isolated countryside. Indeed, there are so few landmarks, the Ordnance Survey has had to mark individual trees on its Pathfinder maps. Dwelly Farm is about the only sign of habitation, followed, the best part of a mile farther on, by Wintersell Farm (10 miles). Shortly after

Barn Owl Kennels, pass the junction of the road to Edenbridge and Marlpit Hill. About two hundred yards after this junction, the road bends sharply to the right and crosses a bridge over the railway. A short downhill dash is followed by a climb, which ends by the half-timbered Grubbs Farm (almost 11 miles).

At the following T-junction – where there's a sign for the Royal Oak pub – the ride turns right but, given the lack of opportunities for refreshment, you may prefer to make the 300 yard diversion to the left to reach the pub.

🍴 *The Royal Oak, Caterfield Lane, near Merle Common. Friary Meux. 01883 722207. Food & Rest*

About 100 yards after the junction, fork left into the lane signposted 'Hurst Green & Merle Common'. Having passed through Merle Common and under the railway, continue straight on past the next turning, following the sign for 'Broadham Green & Tandridge'. This quiet country road, Popes Lane, zigzags its way through the flat, open fields surrounding the upper reaches of the River Eden. Runningwell Stables are at the 12-mile point.

At the T-junction at the end of the lane, turn right for 'Broadham Green, Oxted & Tandridge'. On the right, immediately after the junction, is Stockett's Manor, which is well worth pausing to look at. It's an L-shaped farmhouse dating from the 15th century, although the brick front and Horsham stone roof were added some 200 years later. Outside is an old oast house, once used for drying hops.

There's a gentle uphill climb past the wall surrounding the grounds of the manor (13 miles), the top being reached at Perrysfield Cottage. At the T-junction at the end of the lane, turn right, following the sign for 'Hurst Green & Oxted'. There's a phone box shortly after the junction.

The lane soon comes to Broadham Green Common, a pleasant spot which will repay a pause. From there, turn right into Tanhouse Road, signposted for 'Hurst Green & Limpsfield'. The Haycutter Inn is a short distance ahead on the right.

🍺 *The Haycutter Inn, Tanhouse Road, Hurst Green. Friary Mieux. 01883 712550. Open all day. Food 12–2, 7–10 (Suns breakfast only 10.30–12.30) G Skittle Alley*

Beyond the pub, there's a short stretch where houses line the right-hand side of the road, but open countryside resumes briefly before you arrive at the outskirts of Hurst Green. At the end of Tanhouse Lane (14 miles) there's a phone box and a small, unusual war memorial. (🚉 Hurst Green Station is a short way to the right.)

Turn left into Woodhurst Lane, in the direction of 'Oxted'. The road climbs steadily past a stone wall surrounding a converted oast house called Stone Hamme. Keep going up the hill, past Stone Hall Farm and Broadham Manor, and then turn left into the narrow entrance of Spring Lane. It's not signposted, so take care not to miss it.

The road immediately plunges down a steep hill to Oxted Mill, which has now been converted into offices, and its attractive millpond, which is fed by the River Eden. Old millstones line the side of the road. From the mill, climb the steep hill on the other side of the deep valley.

At the end of Spring Lane, turn right into Beadles Lane, which leads up the hill to the village of Old Oxted, and stop at the crossroads. The High Street served as the A25 until not so many years ago, and congestion can be imagined.

Old Oxted: *Before it was bypassed, one writer described Old Oxted as 'oddly grim; it could almost be a North Warwickshire industrial village'. Another, writing later,*

thought it had stepped out of a Cornish scene, so that he almost expected to see the sea at the bottom of the hill. Were they really talking about the same place? You'll have to decide.

The Old Bell pub dates from about 1500 and is one of the oldest buildings in the village, although it's claimed to have been a 13th century pilgrims' rest-house. Parts of the Crown Inn also date from around 1500, and there are examples of architecture from each of the following centuries in the street. Thanks to the steepness of the hill, many of the houses have stone steps to their front doors, adding further charm. At the foot of the hill the Wheatsheaf pub has its cellar carved out of the sandstone.

In 1975, to celebrate European Architectural Heritage Year, Tandridge District Council produced a series of small, illustrated books covering each of its Conservation Areas. 'Oxted Explored' takes a tour of the High Street, describing each building and its history in turn. It's well worth borrowing a copy from one of the local public libraries.

New Oxted is about half a mile away on the other side of the A25. It's centred round the church and the railway station.

🍺 *The Old Bell, High Street, Old Oxted. Country Carvery pub. 01883 712181. Open all day. G Food Rest (Mon–Sat 12–2.30, 6–9.30, Sun 12–9.30) Carvery all day.*

🍺 *The George Inn, High Street, Old Oxted. Free House. 01883 713453/730656. Open all day. Food (midday–evening) Rest*

🍺 *The Crown Inn, High Street, Old Oxted. 01883 717853. Food C G*

🍺 *The Wheatsheaf, High Street, Old Oxted. 01883 713154. Open all day. Food*

③ Old Oxted to Tandridge

Continue over the crossroads into Sandy Lane, passing under the new bypass. The lane passes over a small brook and then climbs out of the river valley, with Barrow Green Gardens on the left and New Oxted visible to the right. At the T-junction at the

Old Oxted

end of Sandy Lane, turn left into Barrow Green Road. (⇌ Oxted Station can be reached by turning right.)

Barrow Green Court is a Jacobean, maybe Georgian, house, built of mellow brick. Unfortunately, it's hard to see much of it today. Its owner, Mohamed Al Fayed, is extremely security-conscious, and there's a high fence with tall trees inside, closed-circuit TV cameras scanning the road, and German shepherd dogs roaming free inside. In the grounds is the grave of his son, Dodi.

Eric Parker, the noted Surrey writer, thought the Court 'an admirable building'. Barrow Green Farm, next door, he described as 'all that an old farmhouse should be, complete with barns, an oasthouse, and a fascinating front to the road' (see overleaf). The outbuildings have gone, replaced by less picturesque, modern-day equivalents, but the house

remains much in its original condition. Sadly, though, it was left empty for some time, and in 1996 planning permission was granted to build substantial extensions. Opposite the farm is The Mount, a mound 30 feet high and 200 feet in diameter, which, despite its appearance and the name of the surrounding area, is probably natural in origin, rather than a prehistoric barrow.

From Barrow Green, continue along the road past Tandridge Priory (just over 16 miles). The original priory is long gone, its place taken by a private house.

Tandridge Priory, *an Augustinian monastery, was founded at some time in the second half of the 12th century. With never more than five canons (including the Prior) at one time, it was small, even by Augustinian standards. We know little of the history of the Priory. Maybe there wasn't the time for keeping the kind of chronicles which many*

BARROW GREEN FARM.

larger monasteries handed down to us. What records there are show that the Priory went through a spell in the 14th century when its running was most unsatisfactory. Inefficient administration and a lack of spiritual zeal appear to have been the complaints. One problem was that the Priory was poorly-endowed with land and property, and must have had difficulty making ends meet.

The end came in 1536 when, under Henry VIII's Act of Suppression, all religious houses with an income of under £200 a year were closed. Tandridge was worth only £81 7s 4d, and its fate was sealed. The Priory and its possessions passed to the King, who exchanged it for land at Oatlands, near Weybridge, which he intended as the site of a new palace.

The buildings soon fell into decay, and were no doubt plundered for their materials. Today nothing remains of the original Priory except a few stones and the old fishponds.

On the right, after the Priory, is part of the Palmers Wood Oil Field, but don't look for anything on the scale of Texas. One chimney, burning methane from a land-fill site, is all there is to be seen. At the A25 cross over into Tandridge Lane. A gentle climb past a golf course brings you to Tandridge church (17 miles).

📖 *To link with Ride K, turn right along the A25, then take the next on the right, Tandridge Hill Lane. At the top, turn right into Gangers Hill to join the ride.*

Tandridge *is only a small village, but for hundreds of years it lent its name to the institution of government of a wide area of the surrounding countryside. This tradition, which has been revived today through the name of the Tandridge District Council, originated with the administrative system of Saxon times, which divide the country up into areas known as 'hundreds'. Tandridge was at the centre of the easternmost hundred of Surrey, with a meeting place on a low knoll alongside what is now the A25, a short distance west of the village. This knoll is still known by many as*

the Undersnow (a corruption of Hundred's Knoll).

Sir George Gilbert Scott is renowned as the architect of many gems of the Victorian age, including St Pancras Station and the Albert Memorial in London, but he also worked on the rebuilding of many Surrey country churches. Tandridge was one of these – he was responsible for the aisles – not surprisingly, given that he lived at nearby Rooks Nest.

√ Tandridge to Crowhurst

From the church, continue along the lane, reaching the top of the rise by the junction with the delightfully-named Jackass Lane. An exhilarating downhill run follows, with the Barley Mow pub on the left towards the bottom.

🍺 *The Barley Mow, Tandridge Lane, Tandridge. Free house. 01883 713770. Open all day. G Food Rest B&B*

Beyond the pub there's a phone box on the right, just before the village school. At the T-junction about a quarter of a mile after that, turn left into Southlands Lane. Look through one of the gaps in the hedge on the left and you can see Tandridge Court up on the hillside (18 miles). Go past Southlands Lodge, guarding the drive to another large property, and along a level and partly-wooded stretch to the junction with the lane to 'Crowhurst & Edenbridge' at Perrysfield Farm. Turn right here.

You have already covered this stretch of road in the opposite direction, but this time the hill which starts at Perrysfield Lodge (19 miles) is in your favour. At the junction with Pope's Lane keep straight on (signposted 'Crowhurst & Lingfield'), bringing you back into new territory.

This is Gibbs Brook Lane, named after the tributary of the River Eden which it crosses a distance ahead. The river meadows are mostly empty, with only Holly Bush Farm (almost 20 miles) and occasional copses to break the view. The bridge over the brook is followed by a short, but sharp, hill. The next half-mile is more wooded and leads to a bridge over the dead-straight railway line from Redhill to Tonbridge. Turn left at the T-junction immediately after the bridge.

Crowhurst village is ahead. Beyond the village hall (21 miles) is a strange, derelict building on the left which looks like the control tower of a wartime airfield, but there are no signs of such an installation here. The road climbs to the church, opposite which is Mansion House Farm.

Crowhurst is associated with the Gaynesford family, who lived at Crowhurst Place, just to the south, from the 14th century onwards. The church contains the tombs of several members of the family. One, that of Anne Forster, which is to be found inside the alter rails, has an unusual slab made of Sussex cast-iron. Copies of it were made in the form of firebacks, and can be seen occasionally throughout the area.

The earliest parts of the church, which is made of Weald stone, date from before 1200, with substantial later additions. The parish tells how, in 1652, having 'lien in heaps a long time', it had been 'made plain and restored'. It was further restored in 1886 but, fortunately, not to the extent normally associated with the Victorians in Surrey.

Crowhurst is well-known for its churchyard yew tree, claimed to be the largest in Surrey. It's always been assumed that it is at least as old as the church, and maybe older, but recently the biologist David Bellamy estimated it to be no less than 4,000 years old. Until 1850, a fair was held on Palm Sundays under its branches. In 1820, a local publican had the inside hollowed out and benches and a table inserted, with a door to provide access but, by some miracle, it survived.

Another famous Crowhurst family were the Angells, who lived at Mansion House Farm, opposite the church. In the 17th century one

of the family, Justinian, married a daughter of John Scaldwell of Brixton Causeway, hence the name of Angell Road in Brixton today. Another, nearby, is called Crowhurst Road for the same reason.

Mansion House Farm is a delightful building, late medieval in date, but with a late 17th century brick front facing the road.

⑤ **Crowhurst to Lingfield**

Proceed along the road from the church, over a small bridge, and past the junction with Park Road. Follow the signs for 'Lingfield & East Grinstead'. There's a long but steady hill after the junction, which continues past another side turning (22 miles). On the right, about 200 yards after this turning, is the gatehouse of Crowhurst Place. The house itself is about 300 yards along a private drive and, although footpaths pass close to it, the house and the moat which surrounds it are completely hidden by hedges.

Crowhurst Place was built for the Gaynesford family in about 1425 and was a typical example of a hall house of a wealthy yeoman family. Tradition has it that Henry VIII used to stay there on his way to visit Anne Boleyn at Hever Castle, just over the Kent border.

The house was linked to Crowhurst church by a stone-flagged causeway, built in 1631 by one of the many John Gaynesfords. He decided, at the age of 76, that he was too old to walk through the mud to church each Sunday, it being, as the Parish Register put it, 'a loathsom durtie way every stepp'.

When the male line of the Gaynesford family eventually failed (girls were far more numerous among its offspring than boys), the house was sold, and by the beginning of the 20th century it had become a rather neglected and overgrown farmhouse, although one writer described it as 'one of the most picturesque old moated buildings in the southern counties'. The great hall, which had been open to the roof when

Lingfield

John Aubrey visited it in around 1700, had been floored over, but the original roof survived.

During World War I the house was acquired by George Crawley, who restored and extended it almost out of recognition and added the gatehouse, all in imitation of its former style.

From Crowhurst Place the road runs downhill. A sharp left bend is followed by an unsigned turning to the left, then there's a short stretch of road lined by modern bungalows, with a phone box in the midst of them. Farther along, the road crosses the recently-rebuilt Waste Bridge (23 miles), before coming to a junction at Lingfield Common. Turn right then left, following the signs for 'Dormansland & Lingfield'. At the outskirts of Lingfield, fork right into Saxbys Lane, signposted 'Lingfield'. (For the railway station you can continue straight ahead, but we recommend you visit the town centre

before catching your train.) Pass the fire and police stations, heading towards the church. Go straight on into Church Road at the Vicarage Road crossroads, as far as the Star pub (24 miles). Stop here to have a look at the old town centre on the right.

Lingfield: *The small street leading to the church is the ancient heart of Lingfield and must be one of the best historic street scenes in Surrey. On the left, just at the entrance into the street is a house which was once the butcher's shop. Indeed, the front extension was probably built as a shop in the 16th century but, rather sadly, has now been filled in.*

Most of the other buildings in the street were also used for trade in past times. The Old Town Stores is at the churchyard end and, on the right, is the former Star Inn. (Look at the architecture of the front of this building, and then look at the back from Church Road to see how it was modernised.)

The church is a rare example in Surrey of the large Perpendicular style. The tower is 14th century, but the rest was rebuilt by Sir Reginald Cobham of Starborough Castle in the 1430s. His tomb is inside. He also built the college which was attached to the church. The only part of this which remains today is the old guest house, which now serves as the local library, so you can look around inside. The rest of the college was demolished during the reign of George I and a farmhouse (known, confusingly, as The College) built on the site.

▦ *The Star, Church Road, Lingfield. 01342 832364. Open all day. G Food (lunch and eve)*

Continue along Church Road to the crossroads and turn right. At the mini-roundabout turn right into Plaistow Street, then left into Gunpit Road.

Plaistow Street forms today's village centre. Its most prominent features are the pond – now formalised in celebration of the Silver Jubilee in 1977 – and St Peter's Cross, with its attached village cage, standing under the old oak (see photograph on page 136). The cross is said, locally, to date from the 15th century, and marked the boundary between Billeshurst and Puttenham Manors, but it was probably reconstructed in 1773 when the cage was added to serve as a local prison. Used until 1882, the cage seems to have been run on fairly liberal lines in its early days. The door had a grating, through which food, tobacco, and even drink could be passed.

This state of affairs may have been tightened up following the daring escape of a gang of poachers from Copthorne. Their colleagues crept into the village at night, armed with picks and crowbars, and removed the roof!

▦ *The Greyhound, Plaistow Street, Lingfield. 01342 832147. Food Rest*
▦ *The Old Cage, Plaistow Street, Lingfield. Free house. 01342 834271. Patio Food (served all day until late) Rest Acc*

Alternative section of route

① Lingfield to Haxted Mill

☞ *This alternative avoids the off-road section via Dry Hill Fort.*

Leave the car park at Lingfield and turn right out of Gunpit Road. At the mini-roundabout turn left in the direction of 'Dormansland and Edenbridge' (the B2028). This leads into the High Street, which soon becomes Town Hill. Go over the Church Road crossroads and past the end of Station Road, after which the entrance to Lingfield Park racecourse is on the right. Go under the railway bridge and take the next turning on the left, St Piers Lane (1 mile).

The Notre Dame Convent School is on the left a short distance along the lane, but this is overshadowed by the substantial buildings and grounds of St Piers school beyond, which provides treatment, care, and education for 220 children and young people with epilepsy. Founded in 1897, it occupies a site of over 150 acres of beautiful grounds, through which the lane meanders. Beyond the school the lane narrows, and after St Piers Farm (2 miles), it crosses open, low-lying fields. Three-quarters of a mile further on, it meets the road through Starborough. Turn left to rejoin the main route. The diversion cuts 5½ miles off the length of the ride.

Ride K:
Surrey's Forgotten Corner

Botley Hill • Tatsfield • Biggin Hill • Lusted Hall • Beddlestead • Fickleshole • Chelsham Church • Farleigh • Chelsham • Slines Green • Halliloo Valley • Marden Park • Gangers Hill • Botley Hill

Distance: 12 miles to 21 miles
Landranger Maps: 187
Pathfinder Maps: 1191, 1207, 1208

In the far north-eastern corner of Surrey are some peaceful downland villages which are almost cut off from and, some might say, forgotten by the rest of the county. The North Downs are wider here, north to south, than in any other part of Surrey, and there are views and scenery to match. To the south, the Weald stretches out towards the South Downs in the far distance. To the north, much of London is visible, including Docklands with the Canary Wharf tower.

The ride starts on the top of the Downs and remains there for most of the time, so it's not as exhausting as you may think. There's one steep climb on the borders of Tatsfield and Biggin Hill, but you can bypass that if you prefer. There are dips into and out of downland valleys, but you can usually build up enough momentum on the way down to get you most of the way up the other side. But if you do have to walk, at least you'll have more time to enjoy the scenery.

At the end of the ride there's a choice of routes. Each has its own magnificent attractions and they offer, between them, a range of cycling conditions. The route descriptions will help you decide which to follow. You may even want to try the ride several times, choosing a different route on each occasion.

Starting Points

The best place to start is at the Botley Hill car park (grid reference TQ 398554), at the junction of the B269 South Croydon–Limpsfield road with the B2024 to Westerham. There's a car park opposite Tatsfield church but it can be busy on Sundays. There are also car parks at Gangers Hill, the small lane which leads towards Woldingham from the A25 east of Godstone.

⇌ Woldingham station, served by Connex South Central trains on the London Victoria–East Croydon–East Grinstead line, is on the ride. Leave the station by the exit on the London-bound platform and go down the approach road. When you get to the drive through Marden Park, about 100 yards further on, turn left and you're on the route.

Ride K
Surrey's Forgotten Corner

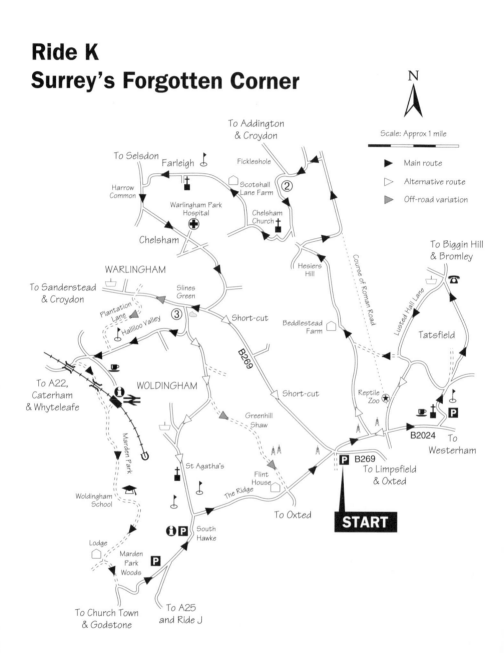

N

To Addington & Croydon

Scale: Approx 1 mile

▶ Main route
▷ Alternative route
▶ Off-road variation

To Selsdon

Farleigh

Fickleshole

Harrow Common

Scotshall Lane Farm ②

Warlingham Park Hospital

Chelsham Church

Chelsham

To Biggin Hill & Bromley

WARLINGHAM

Hesiers Hill

To Sanderstead & Croydon

Slines Green

Plantation Lane

Halliloo Valley ③

Short-cut

Beddlestead Farm

Course of Roman Road

Lusted Hall Lane

Tatsfield

B269

To A22, Caterham & Whyteleafe

WOLDINGHAM

Short-cut

Reptile Zoo

Marden Park

Greenhill Shaw

B2024 To Westerham

St Agatha's

Flint House

The Ridge

B269
To Limpsfield & Oxted

Woldingham School

To Oxted

START

Lodge

South Hawke

Marden Park Woods

To Church Town & Godstone

To A25 and Ride J

The Route in Brief

① Join B2024 Westerham Road opposite CP. TL at next after Clarks Lane Farm, by entrance to Park Wood Golf Club. Pass Tatsfield church and continue SO, SP Biggin Hill & Bromley. At bottom of hill TL into Lusted Hall Lane and climb steeply. At bend 400 yds after Lusted Hall Farm TR through metal gate onto BW. At end of first field pass through gate and continue along edge of field into and out of dip.

Follow track up to wooden gate, then cross field to exit in diagonally opposite corner and TR onto road. At top of hill TR, SP Addington & Biggin Hill. Pass drive to Skid Hill Farm then take next L (unsigned). Keep SO at next two juncs.

② At Fickleshole SO past pub, then take next on R, SP Chelsham & Farleigh. TR at next junc (Scotshall Lane), then SO through Farleigh to Chelsham Common.

TL onto Old Farleigh Road to Harrow pub, then L into Harrow Road. At next junc SO into Ledgers Road, then SO at Chelsham Common Road XR. Pass end of Washpond Lane and continue to B269 Limpsfield Road. TR for about 400 yds then TL into Slines Oak Road, SP Caterham. (See text for alternative routes on next stage.)

③ Continue along Slines Oak Road for about 1½ miles to TJ at bottom of hill. TR (effectively SO) for about 300 yds. Immediately after viaduct THL onto Woldingham School private road (BW) back under viaduct. Follow lane up valley then keep to main drive around school buildings (follow signs for Marden House). At far end of school pass iron gates marked private road.

At South Lodge pass barrier and TL onto rough track. At road TL and climb steeply until TJ with Northdown Road/The Ridge, then TR for 3 miles to Botley Hill.

Downland countryside

The Ride

① Botley Hill to Fickleshole

From Botley Hill head off along the B2024 Westerham road which starts opposite the car park entrance. The road, which is broad and fortunately not too busy, runs along the ridge of the Downs and, if the weather is clear, you should be able to see Docklands and Canary Wharf to the north and a large expanse of the Weald to the south.

Pass Clarks Lane Farm (nearly 1 mile), and then take the next turning on the left. It's not signposted, but it is beside the entrance to Park Wood Golf Club. The lane climbs steeply past the steps leading up to Tatsfield Church.

St Mary's Church, Tatsfield is unusual in being used by both Anglican and Roman

Catholic congregations. At 790 feet above sea level, it's one of the highest churches in Surrey (although St Agatha's at Woldingham disputes this) and there are some excellent views over the surrounding countryside from the churchyard.

The nave dates from Norman times. The chancel was added about 200 years later, although the discovery of some old foundations suggests that it was originally shorter. It was probably extended in the 14th century when part of the south side of the chancel collapsed and had to be rebuilt. The present tower was built in 1837, replacing an earlier timber belfry and spire. The porch and entrance vestibule were added in 1966/67.

☕ *Tatsfield church hall. Tea, coffee, cakes. Sat & Sun, May–Sep.*

From the church go along the lane past the golf course, and down the hill to the crossroads after the village school. Unless you want to go into the village centre (it's

Tatsfield Church

to the left up Ship Hill), continue on the main road in the direction of 'Biggin Hill & Bromley'. The road runs on a shelf along the hillside, as the houses on the left drop away into the valley. Soon there are houses on the right (Little Dene is at the 2-mile mark) and hedges and woodland on the left. Among the large houses are the Old Rectory and the Manor House.

The road now begins to descend quite steeply and is fairly built-up on both sides, although the houses are well tucked away. The resulting effect may not have been contrived but it has been compared favourably with Welwyn Garden City and Hampstead Garden Suburb, where a great deal of effort was put into the planning.

At the bottom of the hill turn left into Lusted Hall Lane. There's a phone box by the junction, and a newsagents around the corner (just under 3 miles). The junction marks the county boundary; the left side of Lusted Hall Lane is in Surrey, but everything to the right is in the London Borough of Bromley, which explains why one side of the road is built-up and the other not.

Tatsfield expanded in the 1920s as neighbouring Biggin Hill and its airfield were developed. Many of its original houses were little more than shacks; a few remain, though much altered. In the days before cars were commonplace, this was a remote spot indeed, more cut-off than it is even today. This was one of the suburban developments around London which did not result from the building of a railway. Maybe speculators hoped to get in before the railway arrived and boosted the value of the land.

A scheme for an 8-mile light railway between Orpington and Tatsfield had been proposed in 1898 but nothing had become of it. An extended version of the project was put forward in 1925; called the Southern Heights Light Railway, it was intended to follow a 15-mile route from Orpington to Sanderstead via

Tatsfield. To keep construction costs low, the line was to have run over the high ground near the church at Tatsfield, but that would have been some distance – and quite a climb – from the majority of homes in the village.

The scheme was privately promoted, but its backers hoped the main-line Southern Railway would take over and run it once it was built. The line was shown on 1920s Southern Railway publicity maps as a 'Proposed Railway', but by the early 1930s it had become clear that the traffic it was likely to carry would never justify the cost of building it, and the idea was quietly forgotten.

As soon as you turn into Lusted Hall Lane you are faced with a very steep climb and most riders will want to get off and walk. There's a fair amount of modern housing on the Bromley side of the road, but the woods on the left make up for this.

By the time the road eventually levels out the houses have been left behind; there are open fields on both sides and Lusted Hall Farm can be seen just ahead. To the left, down in the valley, are some of the old shacks which originally made up the community.

About 400 yards beyond the farm the road bends sharply to the left (nearly 4 miles). Turn right at the bend and go through a tubular metal farm gate onto the bridleway which runs along the right-hand edge of the field inside. The gate is a bit awkward to open and you may find it easier to dismount. The soil in the field is the local speciality called clay-with-flints and, as its name implies, it can be bumpy.

☞ *In very wet weather the clay can be very heavy, so if you'd rather avoid this bridleway, see the alternative route on page K12.*

At the end of the first field, pass through another gate, and continue along the side of the next field and down a steep slope into a dry valley. The way up the far side of the valley is an obvious, if rough, path leading through the trees to a wooden gate. At the top of the slope, the path crosses the line of the Roman road from London to Lewes. There's little sign of it here, but its line is followed by the field boundaries. The line also serves as the county boundary, a fairly common feature of old Roman roads.

Go through the gate at the top of the path and into the field beyond. There may not be an obvious path across the field, there are no signs, and there isn't a way out in sight! So, from the viewpoint of looking through the gate, head half-left towards the far (north-western) corner of the field. As you get closer to it you'll see a track leading out.

Come out onto the road and turn to the right. This is Beddlestead Lane, named after the farm a short distance further on. The farmhouse looks as though it was built in the 19th century, but beneath the surface is hidden a medieval hall-house.

Beyond the farm the road runs steadily downhill through some magnificent rolling downland scenery. Woodland gives way to a large open field on the left at about the 5-mile mark, and then the road plunges into a valley. The climb out, up Hesiers Hill, is quite steep. You may be able to get a run at it, but it seems a shame to speed past all that wonderfully peaceful countryside. You may also miss some sights worth seeing; a nearby wood is called Owls Wood – with good reason – so keep your eyes peeled.

At the top of the climb turn right into Hesiers Road in the direction signposted 'Addington & Biggin Hill'. The road runs for half a mile along the rim of the valley giving some splendid views over the surrounding country. (The 6-mile mark is passed along this stretch.) At the end of this fairly straight and level stretch the

road bends to the left and climbs uphill for a moment. For the next mile the road runs along the course of the same Roman road you crossed a short while back.

Pass the track leading to Skid Hill Farm (signed Whelan Farms), and about half a mile further on (just beyond the 7-mile mark), take the next turning on the left. It's not signposted so keep a good look out. Continue straight on at the next junction and around the bend to the right. Pass Fairchildes Farm and keep straight on again at the next junction – follow the signs for 'Warlingham & Limpsfield'. On the right just after the junction is the White Bear pub.

Fickleshole: The origins of this marvellous name are lost in the mists of time but they're very definitely ancient. A pub, a couple of farms, and the odd cottage are all there is to this tiny downland settlement which, amazingly, is only 5 miles from the centre of Croydon, to which it's connected by the equally delightfully-named Featherbed Lane. The vast housing estate of New Addington is even closer. What a contrast!

The pub gives the game away though. Its car park is clearly intended to cope with the hordes coming from far and wide. Inside, the building has two completely different aspects. It was originally a row of cottages which have been knocked together, and some of the old cottage rooms remain as rustic stone-floored nooks and crannies. However, the rest of the pub has had all the character modernised out of it.

In the dining room is a rare sight though – a Parliament Clock. It dates from 1795 when Pitt the Younger introduced a clock tax. Most inns got rid of their clocks rather than pay the tax and chaos ensued, so special clocks were designed which were exempt from the tax. However, the tax was soon abolished and not many were made. By the 1960s this one was among the last in the country still in working order but sadly that is no longer the case.

The White Bear, Fickleshole

The wooden bear in the front garden once graced the portico of the White Bear Inn in London, which was where the Criterion Theatre now stands. It was brought to Fickleshole when the inn was demolished just after the turn of the century.

The White Bear, Fickleshole. Free house. *01959 573166/572509. Open all day Mon–Fri. Food G C Rest Pets corner.*

② Fickleshole to Slines Green

From the White Bear continue along Fairchildes Road past Fickleshole Farm. About half a mile from the pub the road bends sharply to the right (8 miles); on the left after the bend is an immensely tall laurel hedge. Look to the right across the fields and you can see Chelsham church.

Take the next turning on the right – the signpost, which is well hidden in the hedge, points to 'Chelsham & Farleigh'. The church, just along on the right after a small group of cottages, is in an oddly remote spot, a mile or so from the hamlet of Chelsham. In fact, it was probably sited at an equal distance from the three manor houses it served. So remote was it that a stable was provided outside the lychgate for the visiting priest's horse. It's still there today. Unfortunately the church suffered from heavy 'restoration' in 1870.

Continue along the lane from the church, into a dip and back up the other side, and then take the next turning on the right at the top of the climb (9 miles). The road is called Scotshall Lane, but it may be only coincidence that there are tall Scots Pines by the junction.

For half a mile there is little but woods and fields, then the lane passes Scotshall Lane Farm and Piggeries. A short while after that it comes to open common (about

10 miles). To the left of the road, the tower sticking up above the trees is part of Warlingham Park Mental Hospital. Directly ahead is the hamlet of Farleigh, while to the right the fields have been turned into yet another golf course.

St Mary's Church at Farleigh is tucked away to the left but a signpost points the way from the road. It's only a few yards off and well worth a visit.

Farleigh is yet another downland hamlet which consists of nothing more than a handful of farms and cottages. Although the buildings have been replaced from time to time, things probably haven't changed much in centuries. That includes St Mary's Church. Built in 1083, less than 20 years after the Normans invaded England, it remains in almost the same condition today, despite being damaged by a fire in 1964. Its last real change was in 1250, when the chancel was extended by 10 feet and given a new arch and windows. The porch is Tudor but within it the original Norman arched doorway remains. It really is quite unbelievable.

The church is kept locked but it's possible to arrange to see inside – details are displayed in the porch – and it's certainly worth doing so. Apart from one small electric light, the only illumination is candles.

There's something strange and almost unsettling about standing in a remote hamlet where a tiny church has hardly changed since it was built over 900 years ago and being able to see ultra-modern buildings on the Isle of Dogs just 11 miles away. Two different worlds!

From the church continue along Farleigh Court Road, past Farleigh Court. The water-filled ditches on the left-hand side of the lane are the remains of the moat which once surrounded the manor house. The road dips and winds before bending sharply to the right by the private drive leading to The Chestnuts. This brings it onto the open common and up to a T-junction at Old Farleigh Road. Turn left

but take care because the road can be a little busy at times. At the end of the common is the Harrow Inn (about 11 miles). Look out on the right for a coal tax post (see ride G) just before the pub.

⊞ *The Harrow Inn, Farleigh Road, Upper Warlingham. Bass. 01883 622824. Open all day. Food (all day) G C*

Turn left immediately opposite the pub into Harrow Road. (There's a phonecard telephone box on the corner.) The surroundings are suddenly quite suburban, but not for long. At the next junction, where there's another coal tax post, the huge Warlingham Park Hospital – one of several mental institutions built around the periphery of London during Victorian times – is on the left.

Farleigh church, dating from 1083

Continue straight across into Ledgers Road, passing the turning to the Bull Inn on the right.

📖 *The Bull Inn, Ledgers Road, Chelsham. 01883 622970. Open all day. Food*

Pass a small pond and then go straight over the crossroads at Chelsham Common Road. Just beyond, on the left, is the delightful Old Bull Cottage (12 miles), presumably the forerunner of the modern pub just down the road. The road climbs steadily uphill, passing the end of Washpond Lane, and then, at the top of the hill, bends sharply to the right. About 400 yards further on it comes to a junction with the B269 Limpsfield Road.

☞ *To return to Botley Hill with the least effort, turn left onto the B269 for about two miles. The road is busy and the traffic fast-moving, but there's a path beside it for much of the way which you may prefer to use. On the plus side, the road is mostly level and there are some really marvellous views over the surrounding countryside.*

To continue on the ride, turn right (taking due care) and go along the road for about 400 yards to the junction with Slines Oak Road, which is signposted 'Caterham & Woldingham' (13 miles). There's a pond by the junction.

③ Slines Green to Botley Hill
via the Halliloo Valley & Marden

☞ *The recommended route through the beautiful Halliloo and Marden valleys comes out onto a rough track halfway up the scarp slope of the Downs above Godstone. There's a stiff climb back to the top, but it's worth it, because there are no public roads in the Marden valley, only footpaths and bridleways, so it's unknown to most people. If you'd prefer an easier route, try the one via Woldingham on page 158. It sticks entirely to roads and involves*

some climbing, but mostly at a steady pace, and it's an extremely pleasant ride. Or for something slightly more demanding, see page 159 for the second alternative via Greenhill Shaw which includes a mile of rough track – and a steep climb – over the Downs, but to compensate for the hard work, the views are tremendous.

For the road route down the Halliloo Valley (an off-road variation is given below) turn sharp left into Slines Oak Road. About 300 yards down the hill, follow the road around as it bends to the right and becomes Slines New Road.

The road runs steeply into a dip and back up the other side before descending at a more gentle slope down the side of the Halliloo Valley. In the bottom of the valley is the Dukes Dene Golf Club, the entrance to which is at 14 miles.

☞ *For the off-road variation to this route, continue from Slines Green along the B269 for about half a mile in the direction of Warlingham. Immediately before the Hare & Hounds pub turn left into High Lane and follow it as it curves to the left. Then, just before the entrance to Highlands Farm, turn right into Plantation Lane. This begins as a rough track leading to some houses but soon becomes little more than a path through the trees, most of it in a tolerable if bumpy condition. It runs gently down the side of the valley before curving to the left and dropping steeply towards the golf course, ending near the clubhouse – follow the driveway to the entrance, where the road route is rejoined.*

The Halliloo Valley *is said to derive its enchanting name from an old hunting cry. Until recently the valley bottom was farmland but, despite having been declared a Site of Special Scientific Importance some years back, it has now been turned into a golf course. The valley still retains much of the great beauty which so delighted travellers and writers over* the years, but it's not been enhanced by the artificial nature of the golf course.

Continue down Slines New Road to the junction at the bottom. Turn right onto the main road (effectively straight on), heading towards the railway viaduct about 300 yards further on. Go under the viaduct but, as soon as you are through it, turn hard left onto a private road which goes back under the viaduct. The road, which leads through the Marden Valley to Woldingham School, is signed as a public bridleway. It's easy riding, but watch for the speed humps – they are rather severe!

The road curves gently through some fields before bending under a railway bridge (15 miles). About 200 yards after this, beside one of several park lodges, it is joined by the drive from the rear exit of Woldingham station (once called Marden Park Halt). From here it makes its gently-winding way up this delightful, secluded valley which is now, justifiably, part of an Area of Outstanding Natural Beauty. Pass the turning on the left to Marden Park Farm, and keep going until you get to Middle Lodge at the school entrance.

Marden Park *has a fascinating history. The village which once existed here was wiped out in the Black Death in 1348. In the mid-17th century the land was bought by Sir Robert Clayton, a Lord Mayor of London and, as Macauley described him, 'the wealthiest merchant of London'. Here, in this magnificent setting, he built himself a grand mansion. John Evelyn, the renowned Surrey diarist, visited him there in 1677 and recorded his impressions, 'Tis seated in such solitude among hills as, being not above 16 miles from London, seems almost incredible, the ways up to it are so winding and intricate.' William Wilberforce, the anti-slavery campaigner, was a tenant of the estate. He described it as 'a fine place, one of the prettiest spots that I ever saw.'*

The old mansion was destroyed in a fire in 1879 and a new one was erected on its site

the following year. 'A ferocious Victorian house' is how the Surrey volume of 'The Buildings of England' describes its replacement! In 1906 the Clayton family sold the estate to Sir Walpole Lloyd Greenwell, a stockbroker, who kept racehorses there. When his descendants left in 1946, the estate was split up.

The house became a girl's boarding school called the Convent of the Sacred Heart, which has now become Woldingham School. Nowadays the house is surrounded by a mass of new school buildings and can best be seen by looking back from further up the valley.

Keep straight on up the main drive, around the edge of the school buildings. (The main drive is indicated by the signs for Marden House.) When, at the far end of the school, you come to some iron gates marked 'Private Road', continue straight on (it's a public bridleway). Just beyond the gates the road curves to the right – look to the right from this point and you can see the house of 1880. The road, which is lined by horse chestnut trees, now runs through open countryside, climbing steadily towards the top of the valley. All around are fields of pasture, although one is now a school sports field (17 miles).

At the South Lodge go past the traffic barrier and turn left onto a rather rough and stony track. To the left of the track is Marden Park Woods, which became the property of the Woodland Trust in 1993. If the wind is blowing from the south you'll not be able to avoid hearing the incessant roar of traffic on the M25, even though it's half a mile away at the foot of the Downs. It demonstrates all too vividly the destructive impact modern multi-lane roads have on their surroundings.

Continue along the track for about 500 yards to its junction with Gangers Hill and then turn left. You are immediately faced by a steep climb and a tight bend to the right, and you'll be doing very well if you

Marden Valley

manage cycle up it! Pass Hanging Wood Forest Farm, just after which is another entrance into Marden Park Woods, immediately before the top of the climb (18 miles). The car park at Hanging Wood is a quarter of a mile further on, about 150 yards before the junction with Tandridge Hill Lane.

☞ *To connect with Ride J, turn right down Tandridge Hill Lane. Follow it across the M25 and turn left when you come to the junction with the A25. Tandridge Lane, which forms part of Ride J, is on the right after 400 yards.*

There are tremendous views through the occasional gaps in the trees, which were created by the great storm of 1987. Make the most of the opportunity, because new growth will soon obscure them again. At South Hawke the road bends round a car park. (The conductor Sir Adrian Boult lived at South Hawke and bought parts of the woods to ensure their preservation.) When Gangers Hill ends at a junction with The Ridge (19 miles), turn right.

☞ √ *The alternative route via Woldingham rejoins here.*

Follow The Ridge for nearly 3 miles along the crest of the downs. If it's clear you can see Canary Wharf in the far distance on the left. The views to the right are mostly obscured by the large houses which line the road, but there are a few gaps – look for one beside Rock House.

Opposite the next junction is The Flint House with its walled garden and gazebo, now derelict. Despite its 17th century design, it's actually a 20th century construction.

☞ ⑤ *The second alternative route rejoins here.*

Continue straight ahead at the junction in the direction signposted 'Tatsfield & Warlingham'. At the 20-mile mark, back from the road, is one of the radio stations which take advantage of the heights. After nearly a mile you'll reach the B269 at Botley Hill. Turn right and the car park is on the right.

Alternative sections of route

① Botley Hill to Fickleshole

☞ *This alternative avoids the bridleway across the fields at Lusted Hall.*

Continue along Lusted Hall Lane past the entrance to the bridleway. The road bends sharply to the left and then to the right, passing through a small housing estate,

before joining Approach Road at its junction with Ship Hill by Westmore Green. (The Old Ship pub is a short distance to the left.)

Continue straight ahead into Approach Road and follow it through to its junction with the B2024 Clarks Lane, passing the Reptile Zoo on the way. Turn right, then take the next turning on the right, Beddlestead Lane. Rejoin the main route about a mile along the lane.

③ Slines Green to Botley Hill
via Woldingham (gentle)

From the main road at Slines Green, turn sharp left into Slines Oak Road and go down the hill for about 300 yards. When the main road bends to the right, branch off to the left (straight ahead, in effect) into the continuation of Slines Oak Road, and follow it down the hill past Warren Barn

Woldingham

Farm. Beyond the farm the road undulates and is lined by houses on the right, although they are tucked away in large tree-covered plots and the rural atmosphere is virtually undisturbed.

The road begins to climb gradually towards the village of Woldingham. When you get to the green, turn left into Northdown Road. This heads away from Woldingham (⛯ the village centre, with a good selection of local shops, is in the other direction) and crosses the North Downs golf course. This isn't another of those courses which have sprung up in the last few years and now seem to appear, around every bend of a Home Counties country lane. It was founded back in 1898.

On the right, just before the golf course, is tiny St Agatha's Church. It was rebuilt in flint in 1832 and restored in 1889, but was then replaced by St Pauls, in the village. This was built in 1933 at the expense of Lord Craigmyle.

Beyond the church are Great Church Woods, bought by the Woodland Trust in 1986 with funds raised by local people. Before 1951 they were owned by Sir Adrian Boult, the conductor; he sold them to the Forestry Commission.

A few hundred yards further on the road bends sharply to the left at the junction with Gangers Hill and becomes The Ridge. Here it joins the routes which have come through the Halliloo and Marden valleys (see point ∇).

③ Slines Green to Botley Hill
via Greenhill Shaw (demanding)

From the main road at Slines Green, turn sharp left into Slines Oak Road and go down the hill for about 300 yards. When the main road bends to the right, branch off to the left (straight ahead, in effect)

into the continuation of Slines Oak Road, and follow it down the hill past Warren Barn Farm.

About 500 yards beyond the farm, a gentle S-bend ends with a sharper bend to the right. Turn left onto the rough and stony track which diverges to the left at this bend and heads straight up the hillside. (Parts can be quite muddy after wet weather.) You may find you need to walk, but you'll want to stop anyway to look back at the magnificent view.

The track is broad as it climbs the hillside but as it enters the trees at the top it narrows considerably. Indeed, as it passes through the wooded area of Greenhill Shaw it becomes narrower than most footpaths. Fortunately the situation soon improves and the final stretch, past one of several radio stations in the area, is surfaced.

After about 1⅓ miles the track emerges onto the road called The Ridge beside the wall of The Flint House and opposite the turning to Oxted. Turn left to rejoin the main route at point ⑤.

Notes